职业教育·城市轨道交通类专业
**新形态一体化**系列教材

# 城市轨道交通客运服务英语口语

主　编　胡小依　潘　利
副主编　李　洁　余　莉　毛珺芸
主　审　许迅安

人民交通出版社
北京

## 内 容 提 要

本书为职业教育城市轨道交通类专业教材新形态一体化系列教材。本书从城市轨道交通客运服务出发，内容主要包含了口语对话和常用语句等，旨在培养学生在具有一定的城市轨道交通客运服务知识和客运服务素质的基础上，使用英语向乘客提供优质服务的能力。

本书为职业教育城市轨道交通运营管理专业的专业基础课教材，也可以作为城市轨道交通专业群的拓展课程教材。

本书配套丰富助学助教资源，任课教师可加入职教轨道教学研讨QQ群（群号：129327355）获取。

图书在版编目(CIP)数据

城市轨道交通客运服务英语口语/胡小依，潘利主编.
.—北京：人民交通出版社股份有限公司，2024.9
ISBN 978-7-114-19128-2

Ⅰ.①城… Ⅱ.①胡…②潘… Ⅲ.①城市铁路—轨道交通—客运服务—英语—口语 Ⅳ.①U239.5

中国版本图书馆CIP数据核字(2023)第215505号

Chengshi Guidao Jiaotong Keyun Fuwu Yingyu Kouyu

| 书　　名： | 城市轨道交通客运服务英语口语 |
|---|---|
| 著 作 者： | 胡小依　潘利 |
| 责任编辑： | 钱　堃 |
| 责任校对： | 赵媛媛　魏佳宁 |
| 责任印制： | 刘高彤 |
| 出版发行： | 人民交通出版社 |
| 地　　址： | (100011)北京市朝阳区安定门外外馆斜街3号 |
| 网　　址： | http://www.ccpcl.com.cn |
| 销售电话： | (010)59757973 |
| 总 经 销： | 人民交通出版社发行部 |
| 经　　销： | 各地新华书店 |
| 印　　刷： | 北京建宏印刷有限公司 |
| 开　　本： | 787×1092　1/16 |
| 印　　张： | 10.5 |
| 字　　数： | 264千 |
| 版　　次： | 2024年9月　第1版 |
| 印　　次： | 2024年9月　第1次印刷 |
| 书　　号： | ISBN 978-7-114-19128-2 |
| 定　　价： | 45.00元 |

(有印刷、装订质量问题的图书，由本社负责调换)

### 编写背景

随着城市轨道交通行业的发展,国内越来越多的城市和地区开通了城市轨道交通线路。随着国内外交流的增加,乘客对城市轨道交通车站服务人员提供多语言服务的需求日益迫切。因此,本教材着重培养学生使用英语向乘客提供客运服务的能力和素养。

### 教材定位

本教材是城市轨道交通运营管理专业必修课及专业基础课"城市轨道交通客运服务英语口语"的配套教材。本教材旨在提升学生职业素养、专业理论能力与英语口语水平,培养全面发展的城市轨道交通运营管理专业人才。

### 特色创新

本教材基于乘客进入地铁系统到乘客离开地铁系统全过程,梳理该过程中车站工作人员需要掌握的客运服务英语口语的相关工作任务,确定学习项目(unit),采用"项目导向、任务驱动"的职业教育理念,设置城市轨道交通客运服务英语口语学习领域,使学生能够通过对该领域的学习,掌握城市轨道交通客运服务英语口语相关技能,提高城市轨道交通客运服务能力。

本教材通过对客运服务岗位进行调研,确定各岗位所需要的职业能力,将各岗位所涉及的真实工作任务分解成若干相对独立的典型工作任务,在任务中加入大量对话,让学生在情境中学习,如在进站服务项目中设置进站问询的情境,在进站问询的情境中设置路线问询、购票问询等多个实际应用场景,基于不同场景设置角色扮演任务,让学生在相关情境和场景中,进行英语口语实践,加强口语对话交流能力。

## 主要内容

本教材主要包括站务员服务乘客进站、服务乘客购票及充值票卡、服务乘客进闸、在站台上服务乘客、服务乘客出站、在车站内服务乘客的其他英语口语以及行车值班员英语广播用语,将英语口语与城市轨道交通客运服务结合,培养学生英语口语实践能力,提升学生综合素养。

## 编写团队

本教材由武汉铁路职业技术学院胡小依、潘利担任主编,李洁、余莉和毛珺芸担任副主编,许迅安担任主审。其中胡小依编写了 unit 1、unit 2、unit 7,潘利编写了 unit 3、unit 8,李洁编写了 unit 5,余莉编写了 unit 6,毛珺芸编写了 unit 4。

限于编者水平,教材中难免存在不足,敬请各位读者批评指正。

编 者

**2024 年 6 月**

# 课程思政元素设计

## 整体素质目标

(1) 加强品德修养,培养爱岗敬业的工作作风;

(2) 以人为本,树立良好的服务意识;

(3) 团结同学,培养团队协作能力;

(4) 培养自主学习意识,勇于实践创新;

(5) 增强综合素质,培养国际化的创新思维和沟通能力;

(6) 培养爱国主义情怀,树立文化自信。

### 教学内容与思政内容安排表

| 项目(unit)名称 | 教学内容 | 课程思政元素和内容 |
| --- | --- | --- |
| 1. Entering Urban Rail Transit World | 1. Urban Rail Transit;<br>2. Common Expressions in Metro | 服务意识,文化自信。<br>通过介绍国内外城市轨道交通现状,凸显中国城市轨道交通的先进性,提升学生的民族自豪感、文化自信感 |
| 2. Entering Metro Station | 1. Essential Conversations;<br>2. Prohibited Items;<br>3. Emergency When Passengers Entering the Metro | 服务意识,文化自信。<br>通过乘客进站服务案例培养学生服务意识,通过课后阅读栏目培养学生文化自信 |
| 3. Ticket Service | 1. Ticket Buying Guidance;<br>2. Ticket Sale at the Ticket Booth;<br>3. Ticket Sale at the TVM | 以人为本,团队协作。<br>通过地铁票务服务案例,凸显站务员的以人为本的服务意识,通过情境对话培养学生的团队合作意识 |
| 4. Security Check and Epidemic Prevention Work | 1. Security Check;<br>2. Passengers Taking Illegal Luggage into the Station;<br>3. Epidemic Prevention Work | 团队协作,文化自信。<br>通过思政案例树立学生的文化自信,播种爱国主义情感,通过情境对话培养学生的团队合作意识 |
| 5. Entering the Ticket Gate | 1. Essential Conversations;<br>2. Passengers Can't Enter the Ticket Gate;<br>3. More About Entering the AGM | 综合素质,创新思维。<br>通过站务员解决站台纠纷案例,培养学生遇事沉着冷静的综合素质,启迪学生勇于创新的意识 |

续上表

| 项目(unit)名称 | 教学内容 | 课程思政元素和内容 |
| --- | --- | --- |
| 6. Conversations on Platform | 1. Preserving Order on Station Platform;<br>2. Services under Special Circumstances;<br>3. Platform Accident | 爱国主义,沟通能力。<br>通过爱国案例融入,播种爱国情怀,使学生立志成为有理想、有道德、有文化、有纪律的四有青年 |
| 7. Getting Out of the Ticket Gate | 1. Organization of Passengers at the Ticket Gate;<br>2. Passengers Can't Get Out of the Ticket Gate;<br>3. Passengers Against Regulations | 自主学习,实践创新。<br>通过布置英语趣配音任务,让学生自主学习,培养学生实践创新的能力 |
| 8. Information Service | 1. Passengers Asking for Directions;<br>2. Lost and Found;<br>3. Passengers Asking for Help | 文化自信,服务意识。<br>通过中国文化输出案例,提升学生的民族自豪感,增强文化自信。通过地铁服务案例提高学生服务意识 |
| 9. Broadcasting | 1. Station Daily and Equipment Failure Broadcast;<br>2. Broadcast for Train Delayed | 团队协作、文化自信。<br>通过案例树立学生的文化自信,播种爱国情怀。通过情境对话演练,培养学生的团队合作意识 |

# 目 · 录
## Contents

**Unit 1　Entering Urban Rail Transit World** ·················· 001
   Lesson 1　Urban Rail Transit ·················· 003
   Lesson 2　Common Expressions in Metro ·················· 007

**Unit 2　Entering Metro Station** ·················· 011
   Lesson 1　Essential Conversations ·················· 013
   Lesson 2　Prohibited Items ·················· 018
   Lesson 3　Emergency When Passengers Entering the Metro ·················· 023

**Unit 3　Ticket Service** ·················· 029
   Lesson 1　Ticket Buying Guidance ·················· 031
   Lesson 2　Ticket Sale at the Ticket Booth ·················· 038
   Lesson 3　Ticket Sale at the TVM ·················· 045

**Unit 4　Security Check and Epidemic Prevention Work** ·················· 053
   Lesson 1　Security Check ·················· 055
   Lesson 2　Passengers Taking Illegal Luggage into the Station ·················· 060
   Lesson 3　Epidemic Prevention Work ·················· 065

**Unit 5　Entering the Ticket Gate** ·················· 071
   Lesson 1　Essential Conversations ·················· 073
   Lesson 2　Passengers Can't Enter the Ticket Gate ·················· 078
   Lesson 3　More About Entering the AGM ·················· 083

**Unit 6　Conversations on Platform** ·················· 089
   Lesson 1　Preserving Order on Station Platform ·················· 091
   Lesson 2　Services under Special Circumstances ·················· 095
   Lesson 3　Platform Accident ·················· 100

## Unit 7　Getting Out of the Ticket Gate　105
Lesson 1　Organization of Passengers at the Ticket Gate　107
Lesson 2　Passengers Can't Get Out of the Ticket Gate　111
Lesson 3　Passengers Against Regulations　116

## Unit 8　Information Service　123
Lesson 1　Passengers Asking for Directions　125
Lesson 2　Lost and Found　129
Lesson 3　Passengers Asking for Help　135

## Unit 9　Broadcasting　141
Lesson 1　Station Daily and Equipment Failure Broadcast　143
Lesson 2　Broadcast for Train Delayed　151

## References　157

# Entering Urban Rail Transit World

> Unit 1

城市轨道交通客运服务英语口语

# Lesson 1 Urban Rail Transit

## Part Ⅰ  Warm up

**Discussion**

How many types of urban rail transit do you know? Describe one type of urban rail transit to your partner.

## Part Ⅱ  Words and phrases

metro/subway

monorail transit

light rail transit

maglev transit

urban rail rapid transit system

tram

automated guideway transit system

| metro [ˈmetrəʊ] | n. 地铁 | subway [ˈsʌbweɪ] | n. 地铁 |
| --- | --- | --- | --- |
| monorail transit | 单轨交通 | light rail transit | 轻轨交通 |
| tram [træm] | n. 有轨电车 | maglev transit | 磁浮交通 |
| automated guideway transit system | 自动导向轨道系统 | urban rail transit system | 市域快速轨道系统 |

## Part Ⅲ  Dialogue

**Topic**

Urban rail transit types.

**Dialogue**

Tom is new to Beijing. One day he and his classmate Xiaoming come to take the subway. He is curious about the types of urban rail transit in China, so they ask the station officer.

Tom: The Beijing Subway is beautiful!

Xiaoming: Yes. Metro is one type of urban rail transit in my country.

Tom: How many different types of urban rail transit are there?

Xiaoming: Let's ask the station agent.

Xiaoming: Hello! May I ask how many different types of urban rail transit in China?

Station agent: There are seven types of urban rail transit: metro/subway, light rail transit, monorail transit, tram, maglev transit, automatic guideway transit system and urban rail rapid transit system.

Tom: Thank you very much.

Station agent: You are welcome, have a nice trip!

Tom: The urban rail transit in China is awesome!

Xiaoming: Yes, I feel very proud.

## Part Ⅳ  Speaking

### Task

Create a dialogue with your partner and practice it.

### Topic

Talk about the urban rail transit in your city.

### Reference sentences

(1) When did the urban rail transit start to operate?

(2) How many lines do the urban rail transit have?

(3) What do you think of the urban rail transit in your city?

### Outlines

_____

_____

_____

_____

## Part Ⅴ  Exercise

### 1. Tongue twister

(1) A big black bear sat on a big black bug.

(2) A big black bug bit a big black bear and made the big black bear bleed blood.

(3) A big black bug bit a big black dog on his big black nose!

(4) A loyal warrior wails rarely worry why we rule.

(5) A noise annoys an oyster, but a noisy noise annoys an oyster more!

### 2. Translation

(1) 我国城市轨道交通包含多种类型。

(2) 截至去年年底,北京地铁有多少条线路? 全长多少公里?

(3)中国修建了很多伟大的建筑工程。

(4)武汉目前建成通车了单轨交通。

## Part Ⅵ  Situation dialogue translation

**主题**

城市轨道交通类型。

**对话**

汤姆刚到北京。有一天,他和他的同学小明一起去乘坐地铁。他很好奇我国城市轨道交通有哪些类型,于是他们询问了站务员。

汤姆: 北京地铁真漂亮啊!

小明: 是的。地铁是我国城市轨道交通的一种类型。

汤姆: 那有多少种城市轨道交通呢?

小明: 我们来问问站务员吧。

小明: 你好!请问中国城市轨道交通有哪些类型呢?

站务员: 有7种,分别是地铁、轻轨、单轨交通、有轨电车、磁浮交通、自动导向轨道系统和市域快速轨道系统。

汤姆: 谢谢您。

站务员: 不用谢,祝您旅途愉快!

汤姆: 中国的城市轨道交通真棒啊!

小明: 是的,我感到非常骄傲。

# Lesson 2　Common Expressions in Metro

## Part Ⅰ　Expressions

(1) Let's go to Tian'anmen Square by metro/subway.
咱们乘地铁去天安门广场吧。

(2) You can get almost anywhere rather quickly by subway.
你可以坐地铁迅速到达任何地方。

(3) Look, there're two empty seats over there.
看,那边有两个空座位。

(4) Which platform does our train stop at?
我们坐的那趟车停在哪个站台?

(5) Can we go direct or do we have to transfer?
我们能直达还是需要换乘?

(6) Could you tell me how to go to the platform?
你能告诉我去站台怎么走吗?

(7) Does the train stop at Wangfujing station?
请问列车在王府井站停吗?

(8) How frequent is this subway service?
这条地铁线路发车间隔是怎样的?

(9) Which line do I take to the Art Gallery?
去美术馆乘哪条地铁?

(10) Is this the right subway to go to Jianguo Men?
这是去建国门的地铁吗?

(11) Do I have to pay for an additional fare to transfer?
换乘地铁还要付费吗?

(12) Where do we pay the fare?
我们在哪儿付车费?

(13) Is it the right station to transfer?
是在这一站换乘吗?

(14) Where do I transfer to Beijing Subway Line 2?
请问我在哪儿换乘北京地铁 2 号线?

(15) The train will be arriving soon.

列车马上进站。

(16) Here comes the train.

车来了。

(17) The first train arrives in at 5:00 a.m.

首班列车早上5点进站。

(18) Be careful! Subway doors open and close automatically.

当心！地铁车门是自动开关的。

(19) The train is arriving. Please mind the gap between the train and the platform. Next stop, ×××station.

列车即将到站，请小心列车与站台之间的空隙。下一站：×××。

(20) Please take care of your children and belongings. Thank you!

请照顾好您的小孩，保管好随身携带的行李物品。谢谢配合！

(21) Please be ready to get off as the platform is very busy.

站台乘客较多，请提前做好下车准备。

(22) For your safety, please use our lift if you have a baggage for bulky items. Thank you for your cooperation.

为了您的安全，请携带大件行李的乘客使用升降电梯。谢谢配合！

(23) For your safety, please stand back from the platform screen doors.

为了您的安全，请勿倚靠站台门。

(24) Please move along the platform to the middle of the train for easier boarding. Thank you!

请到站台中间位置等候，那里比较容易上车。谢谢合作！

(25) Please stand firm and hold the handrail when using the escalators. Please don't run or walk in the wrong direction. Thank you!

当您使用自动扶梯时，请站稳，扶好；请勿奔跑逆行。谢谢！

(26) To keep a clean and healthy environment, please don't smoke or litter in trains and stations. Please offer your seats to anyone in need. Thank you for your cooperation!

为了保持良好的乘车环境，请勿在站内及车厢内吸烟，丢弃杂物，乘车时，请将座位让给有需要的人士。谢谢配合！

(27) It will be in a short delay because the last train has not yet left the previous station. Please accept our apologies!

由于列车还未离开上一车站，列车到达本站的时间将出现延误。敬请谅解！

(28) If you're traveling a long distance, please move further inside the train, thank you!

远途的乘客请往车厢中部走，谢谢配合！

(29) Please stand clear of the door. Thank you for your cooperation!
请不要手扶或倚靠车门。谢谢配合!

(30) Your attention, please. Inflammable explosive and poisonous items are strictly prohibited in the system. Thank you!
请注意,严禁携带易燃易爆、有毒物品进站,谢谢配合!

(31) Please wait in line for broading. Let passengers alight first. Thank you!
请按线排队候车,先下后上,谢谢合作!

## Part II  Exercise

### 1. Reading comprehension

With scorching heat waves sweeping across China, cities in Zhejiang Province have adopted a batch of measures to provide more cooling places to residents.

On July 12th, 2023, Hangzhou, capital of Zhejiang, issued its first red alert for high temperatures with the highest temperature at noon exceeding 39 degrees.

Since June 2022, Hangzhou has gradually opened multiple free cool spots for citizens to seek relief from the scorching weather, including subway stations and air-raid shelters.

Starting from July 10th, 2023, the Hangzhou Metro has set up special areas for citizens to avoid the summer heat at its stations. These areas, located alongside seven subway lines with an additional two lines currently in the planning stages, were designed to offer cooling spaces for residents who live near these stations.

Aside from this, the city has also opened six air-raid shelters to the public, which will be open to residents for nine hours each day over the next two months.

(Source: China Daily | 2023-07-13)

**Questions**

(1) What free cool spots has Hangzhou gradually opened for citizens to seek relief from the scorching weather?

(2) How many subway lines are located alongside the areas?

### 2. Translation

(1) 我们一起坐地铁去故宫吧。

(2) 地铁上应该给老年人让座。

（3）请问开往故宫的列车在哪个站台停?

（4）请问去火车站的话在哪一个地铁站换乘呢?

（5）乘客较多,请大家保持秩序,先下后上。

# Entering Metro Station

## Unit 2

城市轨道交通客运服务英语口语

# Lesson 1  Essential Conversations

## Part I  Warm up

**Discussion**

How do you like the entrance of the metro in your city? Talk about the entrance of the Chengdu Metro with your partner.

an entrance of the Chengdu Metro

## Part II  Words and phrases

entrance of metro

ticket center

elevator

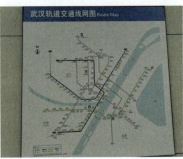

route map

| entrance [ˈentrəns] | n. 进口 | route map | 线路图 |
| ticket center | 票务中心 | elevator [ˈelɪveɪtər] | n. 电梯 |
| passenger [ˈpæsɪndʒər] | n. 乘客 | station officer | 站务员 |
| transfer [trænsˈfɜːr] | v. 换乘 | complicate [ˈkɑːmplɪkeɪt] | adj. 复杂的 |

## Part III  Dialogue

**Topic 1**

Routine enquiry.

**Dialogue 1**

Passengers go to the station of the local line.

Passenger: Excuse me, I'd like to go to Jianghan Road, is this the right station?

Station officer: Yes, this is a station of line 2, you could buy a ticket to the metro station of the Jianghan Road directly.

Passenger: Good, it's so convenient, thanks a lot.

Station officer: Yes it is. When you arrive at the Jianghan Road station, exit from the station at exit A.

Passenger: Thank you very much.

Station officer: You're welcome, have a nice trip.

**Dialogue 2**

Passengers go to the station of the other line.

Passenger: Excuse me, I'd like to go to Jianghan Road, how can I get there?

Station officer: This is metro line 1, you should transfer to metro line 2 to Jianghan Road station.

Passenger: Oh, how can I transfer to metro line 2? Is the transfer complicated?

Station officer: Not at all. You could buy a ticket directly to Jianghan Road station, then transfer metro line 2 at Xunlimen station and take the train in the direction of Jianghan Road station.

Passenger: Yes, thank you.

Station officer: When you get off at Jianghan Road Station, get out at exit A.

Passenger: OK, thanks a lot.

Station officer: You're welcome, have a nice trip.

## Part IV  Speaking

**Task**

Create a dialogue with your partner and practice it.

## Topic

Passengers ask how to get to a destination.

## Reference sentences

(1) I'd like to go to × × ×, how can I get there?

(2) It is a station of line ×, you could buy a ticket to the metro station of × × ×.

(3) You could buy a ticket directly to the × × ×, transfer at the × × × station of metro line 2.

(4) When you get off at the × × × station, get out at exit ×.

## Outlines

_____

_____

_____

## Part V  Exercise

### 1. Reading comprehension

Commuters between Shanghai and Suzhou have a new travel option after Suzhou's Metro Line 11 went into operation.

The new line connects with Shanghai Metro Line 11 at Kunshan Huaqiao Station in Kunshan, a county-level city under the administration of Suzhou, allowing passengers seamless transfer between two cities' metros.

This is the first time that the core cities in the Yangtze River Delta region have linked their subway systems, and is part of efforts to enhance transportation interconnection.

"The most convenient part of taking this new metro line is its flexibility, especially compared with taking the high-speed train," said Meng Fan, a Suzhou resident who frequently travels to Shanghai.

"The metro station is not that crowded, and we will not have to follow tight train schedules. If we change our travel plan at any time on the way, we can just get on and off the metro without too many concerns."

Lu Wenxue, general manager of Suzhou Rail Transit Group, said Suzhou Metro Line 11 was planned as early as a decade ago, when Kunshan Huaqiao Station, which served as the northern terminal of Shanghai Metro Line 11, went into operation.

Shanghai Metro Line 11 connects Kunshan of Suzhou with Shanghai's Jiading district and then continues southeast to pass through the city's Putuo, Xuhui and Pudong districts to end at Shanghai Disney Station.

"Suzhou Metro Line 11 is actually the city's sixth subway route, yet we named it Line 11 in sync with Shanghai's Metro Line 11," Lu said.

According to Ding Chen, an official from the Information Office of the Kunshan Government, Huaqiao is home to nearly 100,000 people who commute regularly between Kunshan and Shanghai.

The launch of the intercity subway line that runs through Suzhou industrial park, and paves the way for further synergy between Suzhou and Shanghai, as many Fortune 500 enterprises have built their Chinese headquarters in Shanghai while placing their factories in Suzhou.

According to published government plans, Shanghai's Metro Line 17, which is being extended to the west, will connect with Suzhou's Metro Line 10 in the coming years.

（Source：China Daily|2023-06-27）

### Questions

(1) What metro line connects Kunshan of Suzhou with Shanghai's Jiading district?

(2) Which subway route is the Suzhou Metro 11 actually?

### 2. Translation

(1) 请问怎么去汉口火车站？

(2) 请问怎么换乘4号线？

(3) 非常简单，您首先购买一张去往武汉火车站的车票，然后在中南路站换乘4号线。

(4) 出站后向左走一百米就到了。

## Part Ⅵ　Situation dialogue translation

### 主题

线路问询。

### 对话1

乘客到达本线车站。

乘客：　你好，我想去江汉路，这个车站对吗？
站务员：　对的，这是2号线的地铁站，您可以直接购买去江汉路站的车票。

乘客： 太好了,真方便,谢谢。
站务员： 是的,当你到达江汉路站时,从 A 出口出站。
乘客： 非常感谢。
站务员： 不用谢,祝您旅途愉快。

### 对话 2

*乘客到达其他线车站。*

乘客： 你好,请问我如何去江汉路?
站务员： 这是地铁 1 号线,去江汉路您需要换乘 2 号线。
乘客： 哦,怎么换乘 2 号线呢? 换乘麻烦吗?
站务员： 一点都不麻烦,您直接购买一张到江汉路站的车票,然后在循礼门站下车换乘 2 号线,乘坐开往江汉路站的列车就行。
乘客： 明白了,谢谢。
站务员： 当你到达江汉路站时,从 A 出口出站。
乘客： 好的,非常感谢。
站务员： 不用谢,祝您旅途愉快。

# Lesson 2 Prohibited Items

## Part Ⅰ  Warm up

**Discussion**

What do you think of the idea of taking a pet on the metro?

## Part Ⅱ  Words and phrases

rail line area

catenary

no pets

no balloon

| | | | |
|---|---|---|---|
| rail line area | 轨行区 | pet [pet] | n. 宠物 |
| catenary [kə'tiːnərɪ] | n. 接触网 | balloon [bə'luːn] | n. 气球 |

## Part Ⅲ  Dialogue

**Topic**

Passengers enter the station in violation of relevant management regulations.

**Dialogue 1**

Passengers enter the station with pets.

Station officer: Sorry. Pets are not allowed to enter the metro station.

Passenger: why?

Station officer: That is because there are too many passengers in the station, pets may cause accidents.

Passenger: I used to see someone taking a dog entering the station.

Station officer: Yes, that's a special case, that passenger is blind, the dog he took is a guide dog, guide dogs are allowed to enter the metro station.

Passenger: Oh, I see. I'll leave now.

Station officer: Thank you for your consideration, you can take other transportations, have a nice day.

Passenger: OK, bye.

**Dialogue 2**

Passengers enter the station with balloons.

Station officer: Excuse me, your balloons can't get into the metro station.

Passenger: Why?

Station officer: The balloons may float into the rail line area and touch the catenary with electricity. It may affect driving safety.

Passenger: What is rail line area?

Station officer: It's somewhere the metro train runs. If the balloons float into it, the train has to get an emergency brake, the passengers in the train will get harmed.

Passenger: Oh, I see. I'll throw the balloon away.

Station officer: Let me help you deflate the balloon and throw it in the trash can.

Passenger: OK, thank you.

Station officer: You're welcome. It's our duty. Have a nice day.

## Part IV　Speaking

**Task**

Create a dialogue with your partner and practice it.

**Topic**

As a station officer, what will you do if you see a passenger taking a bike into the station?

**Reference sentences**

(1) Sorry, we can't have ××× enter the metro station.

(2) There are too many passengers in the station.

(3) The passengers may get harmed.

(4) Let me help you unfold it.

(5) Thank you for your consideration.

**Outlines**

_____

_____

_____

_____

## Part V　Exercise

### 1. Reading Comprehension

Station officer: How many tickets do you want?

　　Passenger: Three tickets to Xidan Station. How much is it?

Station officer: 9 yuan for each.

　　Passenger: Here's 50 yuan.

Station officer: Do you have any smaller change?

　　Passenger: Sorry, I don't.

Station officer: Never mind. Wait a minute, please. (A moment later.) Thank you for your waiting. Here are your tickets and change.

　　Passenger: Thank you.

Station officer: You are welcome.

**Question**

How many tickets does the passenger want to buy?

## 2. Translation

(1)您好,自行车不能带进地铁站。

(2)在某些情况下,可以将自行车带进车站。

(3)车站内乘客众多,我们担心会对乘客造成伤害。

(4)感谢合作,我来帮您。

(5)我们担心气球会进入轨行区,危害行车安全。

## Part Ⅵ  Situation dialogue translation

**主题**

乘客违规进站。

### 对话 1

乘客携带宠物进站。

站务员: 您好,非常抱歉,宠物不能进入车站。
乘　客: 为什么?
站务员: 因为车站内乘客很多,宠物进入容易引发意外事故。
乘　客: 我之前看到有乘客带狗进入。
站务员: 是的,那是特殊情况,那名乘客是盲人,他携带的是导盲犬,导盲犬是可以进站的。
乘　客: 哦,我明白了。那我现在离开。
站务员: 谢谢理解,您可以乘坐其他交通工具,祝您生活愉快。
乘　客: 好的,再见。

### 对话 2

乘客携带气球进站。

站务员: 您好,您的气球不能带进车站。
乘　客: 为什么?
站务员: 气球可能会飘入轨行区,飘到接触网上,影响行车安全。
乘　客: 什么是轨行区?
站务员: 就是列车行驶的地方,如果气球飘进去,列车就不得不紧急刹车,会对列车上

　　　　　的乘客产生伤害。
乘　客： 哦,好的,我明白了,那我把气球丢掉吧。
站务员： 我帮您把气球放掉气后再扔进垃圾桶吧。
乘　客： 好的,谢谢。
站务员： 不用谢,这是我们应该做的,祝您生活愉快。

# Lesson 3  Emergency When Passengers Entering the Metro

## Part Ⅰ   Warm up

**Discussion**

When a large passenger flow comes up, what would you do as a station officer?

## Part Ⅱ   Words and phrases

iron horse

passenger flow control

passenger flow control notice

large passenger flow

| implement [ˈɪmplɪment] | vt. 实施 | accommodate [əˈkɑːmədeɪt] | v. 容纳 |
|---|---|---|---|
| passenger flow | 客流 | emergence [iˈmɜːrdʒəns] | n. 紧急 |
| exceed [ɪkˈsiːd] | vt. 超过 | at present | 目前 |
| Iron horse | 铁马 | limit [ˈlɪmɪt] | v. 限制 |

## Part Ⅲ  Dialogue

**Topic**

Large passenger flow limit at the metro station.

**Dialogue 1**

Organize passenger flow into the station with restriction.

Station officer: Good morning everyone, I am the station officer. Due to the emergence of large passenger flow, the station is now implementing passenger flow restriction to enter the station. Please cooperate with us.

Passenger: What is large passenger flow?

Station officer: At present, there are too many passengers entering the station, which exceeds the number of passengers that the station can accommodate.

Passenger: How to restrict the passenger flow?

Station officer: We will allow passengers to enter the station in batches according to the on-site situation.

Passenger: How long do we have to wait?

Station officer: We can't be sure for now, please line up. We will judge the waiting time based on the number of people.

Passenger: OK, don't keep us waiting too long.

Station officer: Thank you for your cooperation, we will ensure that passengers are able to get in the station and get on the train as soon as possible.

**Dialogue 2**

Passengers complain about the long waiting time.

Passenger: Why not let us get into the station yet?

Station officer: I'm very sorry, there is a large passenger flow at the station, and the passenger flow is restricted.

Passenger: We have been waiting for twenty minutes.

Station officer: Yes, the halls and platforms in the station are currently full of people, the station cannot accommodate more people.

Passenger: We have waited for too long.

| | |
|---|---|
| Station officer: | I'm so sorry. But entering the metro station now is very dangerous. For your safety, please cooperate with us. |
| Passenger: | How long do we have to wait? |
| Station officer: | We've just been informed that passengers outside the station have to wait ten more minutes before entering the station. |
| Passenger: | All right. |
| Station officer: | Thanks for your cooperation. |

## Part IV  Speaking

**Task**

Create a dialogue with your partner and practice it.

**Topic**

As a station officer, you meet a large passenger flow. One of the passengers complains about waiting too long, what will you do with it?

**Reference sentences**

(1) Due to the emergence of large passenger flows, the station is now implementing passenger flow restriction.

(2) At present, there are too many passengers entering the station.

(3) We've waited too long.

(4) The halls and platforms in the station are currently full of people.

(5) For your safety, please cooperate with us.

**Outlines**

_____

_____

_____

_____

## Part V  Exercise

### 1. Reading Comprehension

#### How to buy a ticket with the ticket vending machine?

Using ticket vending machine (TVM) in subway station can avoid long queues and reduce staff's workload. Some passengers are often confused to operate the machine. As a station officer, you are ready to show the whole process to passengers.

Instruction for one-way ticket:

(1)Select the station / the number of tickets.

(2)Insert the coins or cash of 5 or 10 yuan. (The ticket office is available for coin exchange.)

(3)Click the confirmation button.

(4)Take tickets and change.

Instruction for charging:

(1)Click the add value button.

(2)Insert stored-value card.

(3)Insert banknote.

(4)Click the confirmation button.

(5)Take out stored-value card.

Ticket information:

Passengers can use the automatic analyzer inside metro stations to check the information on their one-way tickets, such as ticket fare, validity, and other details.

**Question**

Practice the ticket purchasing process on a TVM with your partner, please following the progress above.

### 2. Translation

(1)为什么不让我们进站?

(2)非常抱歉,目前车站内乘客太多,现在让您进站十分危险。

(3)我们会根据站内人数逐渐让大家进站。

(4)我们收到通知就会让大家进站。

(5)请大家配合我们,这也是为了大家的安全。

## Part Ⅵ  Situation dialogue translation

**主题**

车站大客流限流。

## 对话 1

*组织乘客限流进站。*

站务员： 大家好,我是车站站务员,由于大客流出现,现在车站实行限流进站,请大家配合。

乘客： 什么是大客流?

站务员： 目前进站乘客过多,超过了车站能容纳的数量。

乘客： 怎么限流呢?

站务员： 我们会根据现场情况分批让乘客进站。

乘客： 那我们要等多久呢?

站务员： 现在无法确定,请大家排好队,我们会根据人数判断等待时间。

乘客： 好吧,别让我们等太久。

站务员： 谢谢配合,我们一定尽快让大家进站乘车。

## 对话 2

*乘客抱怨进站等候时间过长。*

乘客： 为什么还不让我们进站?

站务员： 非常抱歉,车站出现大客流,进站限流了。

乘客： 我们已经等了二十分钟了。

站务员： 是的,目前车站内站厅,站台上都挤满了人,车站已经不能再容纳更多的人了。

乘客： 但是我们等的时间太长了。

站务员： 我很抱歉。但是现在进站是非常危险的,为了您的安全,请配合我们。

乘客： 那还要等多久?

站务员： 我们刚刚收到通知,未进站的乘客需要再等待十分钟可以进站。

乘客： 好吧。

站务员： 谢谢合作。

# Lesson 1 Ticket Buying Guidance

## Part I  Warm up

**Discussion**

Do you know where you can buy a ticket at the subway station and how to enquire about the ticket price? Discuss with your partner.

## Part II  Words and phrases

metro ticket

customer service center

ticket enquiry

conductor

| enquiry [ˈɪnkwəri] | n. 询问, 查问 | conductor [kənˈdʌktər] | n. 售票员 |
|---|---|---|---|
| round-trip ticket | n. 往返车票 | one-way ticket | n. 单程票 |
| free ticket | n. 免费票 | welfare ticket | n. 福利票 |
| valid [ˈvælɪd] | adj. 正当的 | confirm [kənˈfɜːrm] | v. 确定 |

## Part III  Dialogue

### Topic 1

Ticket price enquiry.

**Dialogue**

A passenger is enquiring ticket price at the customer service center.

Passenger: How much is the ticket?

Conductor: Ticket price start at 2 yuan within 4 kilometersp; increase by 1 yuan for every 4 kilometers within 4 – 12 kilometers; increase by 1 yuan for every 6 kilometers within 12 – 24 kilometers; increase by 1 yuan for every 8 kilometers without 24 kilometers.

Passenger: Thank you very much.

Conductor: You're welcome, have a nice trip!

### Topic 2

No round-trip ticket selling.

**Dialogue**

When a passenger needs a round-trip ticket, the conductor should explain that there's no round-trip ticket, and offer a solution.

Passenger: Excuse me, I want to go to Jianghan Road. I'd like to buy a round-trip ticket.

Conductor: Sorry, we don't have this kind of ticket at present.

Passenger: Why?

Conductor: The subway doesn't sell round-trip tickets. You could buy a one-way ticket and buy the return ticket at Jianghan Road Station.

Passenger: OK, thank you.

### Topic 3

Free tickets and welfare tickets.

**Dialogue 1**

An old man comes to the ticket booth, showing his senior citizen ID card. The conductor checks whether the ID card is valid or not, and takes corresponding measures.

Conductor: Good morning, what can I do for you?

Passenger: Good morning. I got a senior citizen ID card which can allow me to take the subway for free.

Conductor: OK, please give me your card. I need to confirm the information.
Passenger: OK, here is my card.
Conductor: This senior citizen ID card is valid. You can take subway for free indeed. Please follow me, I will help you go through the ticket gate.
Passenger: Thank you.
Conductor: You're welcome, have a nice trip!

**Dialogue 2**

A passenger comes to the ticket booth and shows his disability certificate. However, after checking the disability certificate, the conductor finds that the certificate does not accord with the rules. The conductor returns it to the passenger and explains the reason.

Conductor: Good morning, May I help you?
Passenger: Good morning, I'd like to get a free ticket.
Conductor: Sorry sir, your certificate is not in accordance with our rules.
Passenger: What should I do now?
Conductor: I'm sorry, you can buy a ticket to take the subway.
Passenger: OK, thanks.

**Topic 4**

Refund the ticket.

**Dialogue**

A passenger wants to get a refund for his ticket. The conductor explains to the passenger that they can't refund the ticket except that the subway is responsible.

Passenger: Hello, I'd like to refund the ticket.
Conductor: Hello, I'm sorry, the ticket can't be refunded.
Passenger: Why not? I bought the wrong ticket.
Conductor: It's OK if you've selected the wrong destination when purchasing your ticket. You could get off at the right station and pay the excess fare at that station.
Passenger: No, I don't want to take the metro now, so I need to refund my ticket.
Conductor: Sorry, according to the subway regulations, ticket refund is not allowed unless the subway is responsible for the issue. Sorry for the inconvenience.
Passenger: OK.
Conductor: Thank you for your cooperation.

## Part Ⅳ  Speaking

**Task**

Make up a dialogue on the given topic with your partner and practice it.

**Topic**

Passengers want to get a free ticket.

**Reference sentences**

(1) How much is the ticket?

(2) Subway fares start at × yuan within × kilometers, increase by × yuan for every × kilometers within ×-× kilometers.

(3) I got × × × allowing me to take the subway for free.

**Outlines**

_____

_____

_____

_____

## Part Ⅴ  Exercise

**1. Reading comprehension**

### The Warm-hearted Station Officer

Passenger: Excuse me! I'm here to thank a warm-hearted staff in this station.

Station master on duty: It is our duty to help every passenger in need. I'm so happy that you're satisfied with our service, but could you describe your experience in detail?

Passenger: Several days ago, I came here to buy a ticket to Hankou Railway Station, but it was my first time to take the subway, so I was quite confused about how to buy a ticket.

Station master on duty: Then what happened?

Passenger: A station officer noticed me and came directly to me, with a sweet smile on her face. She guided me to buy the ticket on the TVM and then lead me to the entrance. Finally, I caught the train successfully. You don't know how grateful I'm to her. She really did me a great favor.

Station master on duty: Thank you for your accreditation. To provide passengers with high-

quality, efficient and warm service, is the pursuit of us.
Passenger: That's great. I sincerely hope you can keep the spirit.
Station master on duty: Of course. Thanks again.

### Questions

(1) Why the passenger is so grateful to the station?

(2) What's the pursuit of the subway?

### 2. Translation

(1) 地铁票价两元起步。

(2) 对不起先生,我们不出售往返车票。

(3) 请将您的证件递给我,我需要确认证件信息。

(4) 你好,我想要换一张免费票。

(5) 请您跟我来,我会帮助您通过闸机。

(6) 对不起,您用于进站乘车的证件不符合地铁公司的规定,我无法为您办理免票服务。

## Part Ⅵ  Situation dialogue translation

### 主题 1

票价问询。

### 对话

乘客站在乘客服务中心前询问票价。

乘客: 你好,请问地铁票价是多少?

售票员: 地铁票价起步 4 公里以内 2 元;4 至 12 公里范围内每递增 4 公里增加 1 元;12 至 24 公里范围内每递增 6 公里增加 1 元;超过 24 公里每递增 8 公里增加 1 元。

乘客: 谢谢。

售票员: 不用谢,旅途愉快。

### 主题 2

无往返车票出售。

**对话**

当乘客需要往返车票等无法提供的服务时,售票员要认真解释,并提供解决办法。

乘客: 你好,我要买往返江汉路地铁站的车票。

售票员: 对不起,目前本站暂时没有这种票出售。

乘客: 为什么?

售票员: 地铁不出售往返车票,您可以购买单程票,回来时在江汉路地铁站购买返程地铁票。

乘客: 好的,谢谢。

## 主题3

免票或福利票。

**对话1**

一位老人到达票亭,并出示了自己的老年证。售票员查验老年证是否有效并采取相应措施。

售票员: 早上好,有什么可以帮您的吗?

老人: 早上好,我有一张老年证,可以免费乘坐地铁。

售票员: 好的,请将您的老年证递给我,我需要确认证件信息。

老人: 好的,这是我的证件。

售票员: 您的证件有效,确实可以免费乘坐地铁,请您跟我来,我会帮助您通过闸机。

老人: 谢谢。

售票员: 不用谢,祝您旅途愉快!

**对话2**

一名持有残疾证的乘客到达票亭,在查验其证件后售票员发现乘客所持证件与地铁规定描述不相符,售票员归还乘客证件并解释清楚原因。

售票员: 早上好,有什么可以帮您的吗?

乘客: 早上好,我想要一张免费票。

售票员: 对不起,您用于进站乘车的证件不符合地铁公司的规定。

乘客: 我现在应该怎么做呢?

售票员: 非常抱歉,但是您可以购买车票乘坐地铁。

乘客: 好的,谢谢。

## 主题4

退票。

**对话**

一位乘客想要退票,售票员应向乘客解释,除地铁的责任之外,其他原因不得退票。

乘客： 您好，我想退票。
售票员： 您好，非常抱歉，不能为您办理退票。
乘客： 为什么不能退票？我买错票了。
售票员： 如果您买票时输入错误的到达站也没关系，您在正确的站点下车后出站补票就行。
乘客： 不，我现在不想乘坐地铁了，所以需要退票。
售票员： 非常抱歉，地铁规定除地铁原因外，其余情况不得退票，给您带来不便请谅解。
乘客： 好吧。
售票员： 谢谢您的合作。

# Lesson 2  Ticket Sale at the Ticket Booth

## Part I  Warm up

**Discussion**

What's your most memorable experience when you bought tickets at the metro station? Share your experience with your partner.

## Part II  Words and phrases

one-way ticket

stored-value card

| change [tʃeɪndʒ] | v. 变化 | destination [ˌdestɪˈneɪʃn] | n. 目的地 |
|---|---|---|---|
| be short of | 不及;少于 | balance [ˈbæləns] | n. 平衡 |
| insufficient [ˌɪnsəˈfɪʃnt] | adj. 不充分的 | put away | 放好 |
| dispute over | 争议 | ticket booth | 售票亭 |

## Part III  Dialogue

**Topic 1**

Ticket sale.

**Dialogue 1**

Passengers are buying tickets at the ticket booth.

Conductor: Good morning.

Passenger: Good morning, I'd like to buy a ticket to Optics Valley Square Station. How much is the ticket?

Conductor: It costs 3 yuan for one ticket.

Passenger: I'd like to buy 2 tickets and here is 10 yuan.

Conductor: OK. Here are your tickets to Optics Valley Square Station and your change 4 yuan, please have a check.

Passenger: Thank you.

Conductor: You're welcome, have a nice trip!

**Dialogue 2**

An old man comes to the ticket booth to buy tickets in cash, but the conductor finds the banknote broken, so she asks the passenger to change another one and explains the reason politely.

Conductor: Good morning.

Passenger: Good morning. I'd like to buy a ticket to Wuhan Railway Station.

Conductor: Sorry sir, this banknote is broken and we can't take it, please change another one.

Passenger: All right.

*The passenger changes another banknote. The conductor takes the money and repeats the destination, ticket price and the amount of tickets.*

Conductor: Here is your ticket and your change, please have a check.

Passenger: Thank you.

**Topic 2**

Short of change.

**Dialogue**

Conductor: Good morning.

Passenger: Good morning. I'd like to buy a ticket to Zhongnan Road Station, but I have no change. Could I trouble you for some change?

Conductor: How much do you want to change?

Passenger: Do you have change for 100 yuan?

Conductor: Oh, I'm sorry, I'm afraid we haven't got enough change here. Please wait a moment, I'll go and get some.

Passenger: OK.

**Topic 3**

Recharge business.

**Dialogue**

A passenger comes to the ticket booth to recharge his IC card, but the conductor finds the banknote is fake, so she asks the passenger to change another one and explains the reason politely.

  Conductor:  Good morning, what can I do for you?
  Passenger:  Good morning. The balance in my card is insufficient, so I'd like to recharge my IC card.
  Conductor:  OK, how much would you like to recharge?
  Passenger:  100 yuan.
  Conductor:  Sorry sir, this is a counterfeit banknote, and we can't receive it.
  Passenger:  All right.

*Then the passenger changes another banknote, and the conductor takes the money and points to the displayer to show the balance to the passenger. After the recharge bossiness is completed, the conductor points to the displayer again to inform the passenger.*

  Conductor:  Now the balance is 101 yuan. Please confirm it. Here is your card and please put it away.
  Passenger:  OK, thank you.
  Conductor:  You're welcome, have a nice trip.

**Topic 4**

Disputes over the ticket price and the change.

**Dialogue**

If a passenger thinks that there is something with the change, the station officer should immediately check. If the ticket and the change is indeed wrong, the station officer should immediately return the money to the passenger and apologize to him. If the ticket coincides with the money, the station officer should also be patient and polite to the passenger.

  Conductor:  Good morning.
  Passenger:  Good morning. I think my change is wrong.
  Conductor:  Sorry, the change is always checked before passengers leave here, please check your change again.
  Passenger:  It is wrong indeed. I've bought 2 tickets, which cost me 4 yuan, and I gave you 10 yuan. The change should be 6 yuan, but you gave me too little change—I only got 1 yuan.
  Conductor:  Please wait a moment. we'll stop to check immediately.

*The conductor checks again and finds out the change is wrong indeed. Then he gives the rest of the change to the passenger and apologizes to him.*

Conductor: I'm very sorry to bring you inconvenience because of my mistake. I sincerely hope you could forgive me. It will never happen again, and this is your change, please check again.

Passenger: All right.

## Part IV  Speaking

**Task**

Make up a dialogue on the given topic with your partner and practice it.

**Topic**

Passengers want to recharge their IC card.

**Reference sentences**

(1) The balance in my card is insufficient.

(2) I want to recharge × yuan.

(3) Please confirm it.

**Outlines**

_____

_____

_____

_____

## Part V  Exercise

**1. Reading comprehension**

### The Customer Service Center

The customer service center is the brand window of subway service image, and is very important. In China, it can be seen in almost every metro station, which is usually located at the center or the end of the waiting hall. Aimed at providing excellent service and meeting the needs of passengers, the function of the customer service center in metro stations mainly focuses on dealing with various affairs such as ticket sale, complaints handling, station hall inspection, etc.

**Questions**

(1) Why the customer service center is so important?

(2) What are the functions of the customer service center in metro stations?

## 2. Translation

(1) 这是您到光谷广场站的票和您的找零。

(2) 对不起先生,请您换一张纸币。

(3) 对不起,我没有零钱了,您有零钱吗?

(4) 这是您的卡和找零。

(5) 我的卡内余额不足,想要充值。

# Part VI  Situation dialogue translation

### 主题 1

售票。

### 对话 1

乘客在乘客服务中心买票。

售票员: 早上好。

乘客: 早上好。我要买到光谷广场站的车票。票价多少?

售票员: 单张票价 3 元。

乘客: 我要买 2 张票,这是 10 元钱。

售票员: 好的。给您 2 张到光谷广场站的单程票和找零的 4 元,请您查点。

乘客: 谢谢。

售票员: 不用谢,祝您旅途愉快!

### 对话 2

一位老人前往票亭使用现金购票。售票员发现纸币有破损,于是委婉地向乘客解释并请乘客换张纸币。

售票员: 早上好。

乘客: 早上好。我要买到武汉火车站的地铁票。

售票员: 对不起,这张钞票有破损,我们无法接收,请您更换一张钞票。

乘客: 好吧。

乘客更换了另一张纸币,售票员接过纸币,并且再次重复目的地、票价和数量。

售票员: 这是您的车票和找零,请您查点。

乘客： 谢谢。

## 主题 2

零钱不足。

**对话：**

售票员： 早上好。

乘客： 早上好。我想要买一张到中南路地铁站的车票，但是我没有零钱，请问我能麻烦您帮我换一点零钱吗？

售票员： 请问您需要换多少钱的零钱呢？

乘客： 你能把一百块兑换成零钱吗？

售票员： 非常抱歉，我这里的零钱不够，请您稍等，我去拿一些零钱过来。

乘客： 好的。

## 主题 3

充值业务。

**对话**

一位乘客到票亭办理现金充值业务，但是工作人员发现现金是假钞，于是她请乘客换一张纸币，并有礼貌地进行解释。

售票员： 早上好。请问有什么我可以帮您的？

乘客： 早上好。我卡内余额不足，想要充值。

售票员： 请问您想要充值多少呢？

乘客： 一百元。

售票员： 很抱歉，这是一张假币，我们不能收。

乘客： 好吧。

乘客换了一张纸币，售票员接过纸币，并且用手指向屏幕告知乘客卡内余额，充值完毕后再次用手指向显示器告知乘客充值完毕。

乘客： 是的。

售票员： 现在卡内余额 101 元，请您确认。这是您的卡，请您收好。

乘客： 谢谢。

售票员： 不用谢，祝您旅途愉快！

## 主题 4

票款不符导致纠纷。

**对话**

当乘客认为票款不符时，工作人员应立即进行核查。若的确是工作人员的失误，工作人员应马上把钱退还给乘客，并向乘客道歉。若票款一致，工作人员仍要耐心、礼貌地向乘客解释。

售票员： 早上好。

乘客： 早上好,我觉得我的找零有问题。

售票员： 对不起,我们的票款是当面点清的,请您再确认一下您的找零。

乘客： 票款确实不对。我买了两张票,费用 4 元。我给您 10 元,找零应该是 6 元,但您少给我找了零钱——我只收到了 1 元。

售票员： 好的,请您稍等,我们立即进行核查。

售票员发现票款确实有误,随后他将零钱归还乘客并向其道歉。

售票员： 对不起,由于我工作的疏忽给您带来了不便,希望得到您的谅解。以后不会再发生这种情况了,这是找您的钱款,请您点收。

乘客： 好的。

# Lesson 3  Ticket Sale at the TVM

## Part I  Warm up

**Discussion**

Do you know how to buy a ticket on the ticket vending machine? Share your experience with your partner.

## Part II  Words and phrases

ticket vending machine (TVM)

out of service

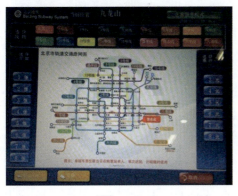

AFC screen

slot

| line up | 排队 | for the sake of | 为了 |
|---|---|---|---|
| wait for | 等候 | slot [slɑːt] | n. 投币口 |
| maintenance [ˈmeɪntənəns] | n. 维护; | cylinder [ˈsɪlɪndər] | n. 圆柱体 |
| seek help from | 向…寻求帮助 | out of service | 暂停使用 |

## Part III  Dialogue

### Topic 1

Guide passengers to line up at the less crowded TVM.

**Dialogue**

When there are many passengers in front of the ticket booth, station staff should get them to stay in a line.

Station officer: Ladies and gentlemen, please line up so that all of you can get the ticket faster.

*The station officer finds that some passengers are standing in line with 5 yuan, 10 yuan, and 20 yuan, then she guides these passengers to buy tickets on the ticket vending machine where are less crowded.*

Station officer: Good morning.

Passenger: Good morning.

Station officer: The ticket booth is full of passengers and I saw that you've got the change. For the sake of your time, please buy your ticket on the ticket vending machine.

Passenger: There are also many passengers waiting in line in front of the TVM. I don't want to go there.

Station officer: The TVM over there is less crowded, and it's more convenient for you to buy the ticket there, which will greatly save your time.

Passenger: OK, I'll try. Where is it?

Station officer: Go across the hall and you can see it. You will not miss it.

Passenger: Thank you.

### Topic 2

The procedure of buying tickets on the TVM.

**Dialogue**

Station officer: Good morning. What can I do for you?

Passenger: Good morning. I need to buy a metro ticket, but I don't know how to handle this machine. Can you buy one for me?

Station officer: Sorry, I can't buy the ticket for you, but I can teach you how to use the machine.

Passenger: OK.

Station officer: First, choose the destination and confirm the ticket price.

*The station officer watches and waits for the passenger to handle the TVM.*

Station officer: All right, now, please put 5 yuan (or 10 yuan or coins) into the machine on the slot.

*The passenger does what the officer says, but the cash keeps being returned back by the machine, so the passenger seeks help from the station officer. The station officer and the passenger try to smooth the cash, but it still can't get through.*

Passenger: I can't buy the ticket because that machine keeps returning my money back.

Station officer: Please wait a minute. Let me check. Maybe your money is too old, so the machine can't recognize it. Change another one and try again please.

*The passenger takes out a new 5-yuan banknote, and the TVM successfully recognizes it.*

Passenger: All right, it works now. What's next?

Station officer: Now, you can get your ticket and the change.

Passenger: Thank you.

Station officer: You're welcome, have a nice trip!

## Topic 3

Guidance during equipment maintenance and repairing.

### Dialogue 1

The TVM needs to change ticket cylinder and cash box.

Station officer: Excuse me, sir. Are you going to buy a ticket?

Passenger: Yes. What's wrong?

Station officer: Sorry sir, this machine needs to change ticket cylinder and cash box, so it will be temporarily closed. Please wait or use another machine, thank you.

Passenger: OK.

Station officer: Thank you for your understanding and cooperation.

### Dialogue 2

Equipment failures.

*When a passenger fails to handle the machine because equipment failures, the station officer should guide the passenger to buy tickets on another TVM, and hang up the Out of Service notice.*

Station officer: Excuse me. Are you going to buy a ticket?

Passenger: Yes. What's wrong?

Station officer: Sorry, there's something wrong with this machine, so it will be temporarily closed, please use another machine, thank you.

Passenger: OK.

Station officer: Thank you for your understanding and cooperation.

## Part Ⅳ  Speaking

**Task**

Make up a dialogue on the given topic with your partner and practice it.

**Topic**

Some passengers want to buy tickets, but the TVM suddenly breaks down. As the station officer on duty, you should comfort and guide the passengers.

**Reference sentences**

(1) There's something wrong with this machine, so it will be temporarily closed.

(2) This machine needs to change ticket cylinder and cash box.

(3) I will hang up the *Out of Service* notice.

**Outlines**

_____

_____

_____

_____

## Part Ⅴ  Exercise

### 1. Reading comprehension

#### The Warm-hearted Station Officer

Passenger: Excuse me!

Station officer: What can I do for you, sir?

Passenger: I want to buy a ticket to Hanzheng Road Station, but I have no change except for 100 yuan.

Station officer: Sorry sir, now we don't have enough change. You can apply for a stored-value card.

Passenger: I'm a visitor from Sichuan province, and I'm going to travel in Wuhan for only three days, so a stored-value card is unnecessarily. Can I use swipe QR code to pay for the ticket?

Station officer: Yes, you can. QR codes have been implemented in many cities, and so has Wuhan Metro.

Passenger: Oh, that's great. Wuhan Metro has made an astonishing progress and the quality of development is quite high. It's remarkable for Wuhan Metro to keep up with the information age.

Station officer: Thank you for your compliment. Wish you have a pleasant visit in Wuhan!

**Questions**

(1) Have QR codes been implemented in Wuhan?

(2) What's the passenger's attitude towards Wuhan Metro?

**2. Translation**

(1) 选择您的目的地,确认票价。

(2) 请从投币口投入 5 元。

(3) 我看见您已经有零钱了,为了节约时间,请用自动售票机买票,那里没那么拥挤。

(4) 这台设备需要更换票筒和票箱,暂停使用。

(5) 您的钱太旧,所以机器无法识别。

## Part VI　Situation dialogue translation

**主题 1**

引导乘客前往人数较少的自动售票机购票。

**对话**

当票亭前面排起长队时,站务员应引导乘客排队。

站务员：女士们先生们,为了您能更快买到车票,请自觉排队。

站务员发现有乘客手持 5 元、10 元、20 元零钱,随后她引导这些乘客前往人数较少的自动售票机购票。

站务员：早上好。

乘客：早上好。

站务员：乘客服务中心人数较多,我看到您有零钱,为了节约时间,请您到自动售票机处购买车票。

乘客： 但是这台自动售票机前面仍然有很多人在排队,我不想去那里买票。
站务员： 那边的自动售票机处人数较少,到那边买票更方便,会节约您的时间。
乘客： 好吧,我试一试。你说的那台自动售票机在哪里?
站务员： 您穿过大厅就可以看见,您一定不会错过它的。
乘客： 谢谢。

**主题 2**

在自动售票机上购票的步骤。

站务员： 早上好。请问有什么我可以帮您的?
乘客： 早上好。我需要买一张地铁票,但是我不知道怎么使用这台机器,请问你能帮我买票吗?
站务员： 对不起,我不能帮您买票,但是我可以教您如何使用自动售票机。
乘客： 好的。
站务员： 首先选择您的目的地,确认票价。

站务员观看并等待乘客操作设备。

站务员： 现在请将 5 元(或 10 元)纸币或硬币从投币口投入。

乘客按照站务员的指导进行操作,但是纸币多次被机器退出,于是乘客继续向站务员寻求帮助。站务员和乘客试图将纸币展平,但仍无法通过机器。

乘客： 我的钱币总是被机器退出,没有办法买票。
站务员： 请等一下。让我检查一下。有很有可能是因为您的这张钞票太旧了,机器无法识别。你换一张钞票试试吧。

乘客拿出新的 5 元钞票。机器成功识别了这张钞票。

乘客： 好的,现在成功了。下一步是什么?
站务员： 现在您可以收好您的车票和零钱了。
乘客： 谢谢。
售票员： 不用谢,祝您旅途愉快!

**主题 3**

设备日常维护或维修时的引导语。

**对话 1**

自动售票机需要更换票筒和钱箱。

站务员： 早上好。请问您是否要买票?
乘客： 是的。怎么了?
站务员： 对不起,这台设备需要更换票筒和钱箱,暂停使用。请您耐心等待或请使用其他设备,谢谢。
乘客： 好的。

站务员： 谢谢您的理解和支持。

**对话 2**

*设备出现故障。*

*当乘客使用的机器出现故障时，站务员应该立即挂暂停服务牌并请乘客使用另一台机器。*

站务员： 早上好。请问您是否要买票？

乘客： 是的，怎么了？

站务员： 对不起，这台设备出现故障，暂停使用。请您使用其他设备，谢谢。

乘客： 好的。

站务员： 谢谢您的理解和支持。

# Security Check and Epidemic Prevention Work

Unit 4

城市轨道交通客运服务英语口语

# Lesson 1  Security Check

## Part I   Warm up

**Discussion**

You are a station officer. While you are at duty, you see a passenger at the security check refuses to check her bag, and yell at the inspector, what would you do?

## Part II   Words and phrases

security check              inspector

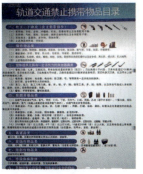          

rules of subway              subject belt

| security check | 安检 | inspector [ɪnˈspektər] | 安检员 |
| --- | --- | --- | --- |
| rule of subway | 地铁规定 | prohibit [prəˈhɪbɪt] | 禁止 |
| subject belt | 传送带 | screen [skriːn] | 扫描 |

## Part Ⅲ  Dialogue

**Topic**

Security check guide.

**Dialogue 1**

A passenger is unwilling to put his suitcase on the belt.

Inspector: Good morning, please put all your belongings on the subject belt for security check.

Passenger: No, your machine is very dirty.

*The station officer found the passenger unwilling to do the security check, then he goes to talk to the passenger.*

Station officer: I'm sorry, for your and other passengers' security, we need to check your belongings, please cooperate with us.

Passenger: There is nothing dangerous in my bag. I don't need security check.

Station officer: Sorry, we don't accept the words that you said about your bag. We must check your bag with the machine no matter what you have in your bag according to the subway rules which are made to ensure your and other passengers' security.

Passenger: OK.

Station officer: Thank you for your cooperation. Please put your package on the subject belt, it will be screened by the machine.

*Then this passenger put his package on the subject belt. After it has passed the machine, the inspector returns it to the passenger.*

Passenger: Thank you.

Inspector: You're welcome. Thank you for your cooperation.

**Dialogue 2**

A passenger is unwilling to put his suitcase on the belt and only willing to check by opening his bag.

Inspector: Good morning sir, please put all your belongings on the subject belt for security check.

Passenger: No, I'd rather not, I will open my bag for you to check.

*A station officer founds the passenger is unwilling to do security check, so he comes up and talks to the passenger.*

Station officer: I'm sorry, for your and other passengers' security, we need to check your belongings on the machine. Please cooperate with us.

Passenger: You could look over my bag directly.

Station officer: Sorry. Lots of prohibited goods can't be recognized by eyes. We must check every passenger's bag with the machine to ensure safety according to the subway rules which are made to ensure your and other passengers' security.

Passenger: All right.

Station officer: Thank you for your cooperation. Please put your package on the subject belt, It will be screened by the machine.

*Then this passenger puts his package on the subject belt. After it has passed the machine, the inspector returns it to the passenger.*

Passenger: Thank you very much.

Inspector: You're welcome. Thank you for your cooperation.

## Part IV  Speaking

**Task**

Create a dialogue with your partner and practice it.

**Topic**

A passenger wants to go through the security check without checking his bag and shouting: I'm in a hurry! Excuse me please. As a station officer, what would you do with it?

**Reference sentences**

(1) Please put all your belongings on the subject belt for security check.

(2) For your and other passengers' security, we will check your belongings on the machine. Please cooperate with us.

(3) We don't accept the words that you said about your bag.

(4) It is made to ensure your and other passengers' security.

**Outlines**

_____

_____

_____

## Part V　Exercise

### 1. Reading Comprehension

Qingdao metro Line 1, the first subway that goes undersea, connects Qingdao and Huangdao, lining up five districts in between. It connects the city transportation network with Line 2 and Line 3.

A total of 39 stations are established along Line 1. The average distance between two stations is 1,567 meters, the farthest is 7,775 meters and the shortest is 740 meters. There are two subway bases: one parking lot and one control center along the line.

（Source：China Daily|2013-08-26）

**Questions：**

（1）What is the first subway that goes undersea in Qingdao?

（2）How many stations are established along Line 1?

### 2. Translation

（1）乘客您好,请安检。

（2）为了您的安全,请配合我们进行安检。

（3）您的随身物品需要通过安检机检查。

（4）地铁安检必须通过安检机,这也是为了所有乘客的安全。

（5）谢谢您的配合。这是您的包,请拿好。

## Part VI　Situation dialogue translation

**主题**

引导安检。

**对话 1**

乘客在进站时,不愿将物品放入安检机。

安检员： 乘客您好,请将您的个人物品放到传送带上进行安检。

乘客：　不，你的安检机太脏了。

*站务员发现乘客不愿意将物品放上安检机。他过去与乘客沟通。*

站务员：　抱歉，为了您和他人的共同安全，我们要对每一位乘客所携带的物品进行安检，请配合我们的工作。

乘客：　我的包里没有任何危险物品。我不需要安检。

站务员：　对不起，您口头上说您的行李没有问题，我们是不接受的。我们必须用安检机检查您的行李，无论您的包里有什么。这是我们地铁的规定，也是为了您和其他乘客的安全。

乘客：　好吧。

站务员：　谢谢合作。请把您的随身物品放到传送带上，安检机会扫描。

*该名乘客将随身物品放到传送带上。物品通过安检机后，安检员将物品还给乘客。*

乘客：　谢谢。

安检员：　不用谢。谢谢你的合作。

## 对话2

*乘客在进站时，不愿将物品放入安检机，只同意开包检查。*

安检员：　乘客您好，请将您的个人物品放到传送带上进行安检。

乘客：　我不想把我的包放到传送带上。我把包打开让你检查吧。

*站务员发现乘客不愿意将物品放上安检机，过来与乘客沟通。*

站务员：　对不起，为了您和他人的共同安全，我们要对每一位乘客所携带的物品进行安检，请配合我们的工作。

乘客：　你直接看我的包里的东西就行。

站务员：　对不起，很多不能携带进入地铁的物品靠肉眼是无法识别的。每一位乘客的随身物品必须通过安检机才能确定是否安全。这是我们地铁的规定，也是为了您和其他乘客的安全。

乘客：　好吧。

站务员：　谢谢合作，请把您的随身物品放到传送带上，安检机会进行扫描。

*该名乘客将随身物品放到传送带上。物品通过安检机后，安检员将物品归还。*

乘客：　谢谢。

安检员：　不用谢。谢谢你的合作。

# Lesson 2  Passengers Taking Illegal Luggage into the Station

## Part I  Warm up

**Discussion**

What items do you think cannot pass the metro security check?

禁止携带下列物品
THE FOLLOWING OBJECTS IS NOT PERMITTED

枪支 FIREARMS　　弹药 AMMUNITION　　警械 POLICEWEAPONS　　管制刀具 CONTROLED KNIFE　　放射物品 RADIOACTIVE

易燃易爆 FLAMMABLE EXPLOSIVES　　腐蚀品 CORROSIVES　　毒害品 POISONS　　氧化剂 OXIDISING　　强磁物品 MAGNETIZED

## Part II  Words and phrases

flammable sign

wrench

| flammable [ˈflæməbl] | adj. 易燃的 | wrench [rentʃ] | n. 扳手 |
| hairspray [ˈherspreɪ] | n. 发胶 | explosive [ɪkˈsploʊsɪv] | adj. 易爆的 |
| stipulate [ˈstɪpjuleɪt] | vt. 规定 | toxic [ˈtɑːksɪk] | adj. 有毒的 |

Security Check and Epidemic Prevention Work   Unit 4

## Part Ⅲ   Dialogue

**Topic**

Passengers take prohibited items getting through security check.

**Dialogue 1**

A passenger carrying hairspray through security check.

Inspector: Sorry to disturb you. Please open the package to check.
Passenger: Why?
Station officer: We found that there are flammable and explosive items in your bag.
Passenger: No way!
Station officer: Do you bring hairspray?
Passenger: Yes. Is hairspray prohibited?
Station officer: Hairspray is flammable and explosive, and the subway strictly stipulates that such items are not allowed to enter the station.

*The passenger takes out the hairspray, and the station officer points to the flammable sign on the hairspray bottle.*

Station officer: See, items with this flammable mark cannot be brought into the subway.
Passenger: Oh, sorry, my fault.
Station officer: It's okay. Please remember not to bring flammable, explosive, toxic and regulated knives to the subway.
Passenger: OK, I see.
Station officer: Thank you for your cooperation.
Passenger: That's all right.

**Dialogue 2**

Passengers carry extra-long items.

IInspector: I'm sorry. According to the Guangzhou Metro safety regulation, you shouldn't carry any extra-long items that can be harmful to the passengers.
Passenger: I will be careful, OK?

*The station master on duty watches this and comes up to deal with it.*

Station master on duty: This concerned about passengers' safety. We can't be more cautious.
Passenger: Why don't you tell me earlier?
Station master on duty: Each exit has relevant rules on the wall. Maybe you haven't noticed. Have you bought a ticket?

| | |
|---|---|
| Passenger: | Yes. What should I do now? |
| Station master on duty: | You can get a refund for your ticket. Is it OK? |
| Passenger: | No. The glass is very heavy. It's hard to carry it in the station. |
| Station master on duty: | OK, we'll ask a staff help you to carry out the glass. |
| Passenger: | But I really want to take the subway. |
| Station master on duty: | I'm sorry. But this concerns your and other passengers' safety. Please cooperate with us. |
| Passenger: | OK, I'll take a bus. |
| Station master on duty: | Thank you for your understanding and cooperation. |

## Part Ⅳ  Speaking

### Task

Create a dialogue with your partner and practice it.

### Topic

A passenger gets through the security check and takes a perfume with her. As a station officer, what will you do with it?

### Reference sentences

(1) We find that there are flammable and explosive items in your bag.

(2) Do you bring perfume?

(3) Perfume is flammable and explosive.

(4) You can get a refund for your ticket. Is it OK?

(5) Please remember not to bring flammable, explosive, toxic and regulated knives to the subway.

### Outlines

_____

_____

_____

_____

## Part Ⅴ  Exercise

### 1. Reading comprehension

On Monday afternoon, four express boxes were transported through Beijing Subway line 4. The boxes were loaded at National Library Station and unloaded at Haidian Huangzhuang Station.

On the train, they were placed on the vacant space at the back of the last carriage, escorted by a subway security worker.

The capital city kicked off the pilot project of using urban rail transit to transport parcels on Saturday during off-peak hours, the first of its kind in the country, aiming to improve utilization efficiency of urban rail transit resources, alleviate urban traffic congestion and lower carbon emissions, according to the Beijing Municipal Commission of Transport.

The express boxes get on the train at the stations of Xidan, National Library and Weigongcun, and get off at Haidian Huangzhuang at around 12:30 p.m. and 15:30 p.m. on weekdays.

The subway line 9-Fangshan line-Yanfang line pilot program kicked off on Saturday to transport newspapers by China Post. The papers were loaded at Liuliqiao Station of line 9 at 9 a.m., when the average load factor of the train was lower than 20 percent, and were unloaded at Yanshan Station.

(Source: China Daily | 2023-09-25)

**Questions**

(1) Where were the boxes loaded on the train?

(2) Where were the newspapers loaded?

**2. Translation**

(1) 打扰一下。您的包里可能携带了违禁品。请接受开包检查。

(2) 是的，这是违禁品。瓶子上标有易燃物的就不能带进地铁车站乘车。

(3) 易燃易爆、有毒物品不能带进地铁车站。

(4) 您好。您的物品超长了，不能带进车站。请乘坐其他交通公交工具。

(5) 给您办理退票可以吗？

## Part Ⅵ　Situation dialogue translation

**主题**

乘客携带违禁品过安检。

## 对话 1

*乘客携带发胶过安检。*

安检员：对不起，打扰一下。请开包检查。
乘客：为什么呢？
安检员：我们发现您的包里有易燃易爆物品。
乘客：不可能。
站务员：您是不是携带了发胶？
乘客：是的。发胶是违禁品？
站务员：发胶属于易燃易爆物品，地铁严格规定不得携带该类物品进站乘车。

*乘客掏出了发胶。站务员指着发胶瓶上的易燃物标志。*

站务员：您看，带有这种易燃物标志的物品都不能带入地铁的。
乘客：哦，对不起，我的错。
站务员：没关系，请记住乘坐地铁时请勿携带易燃易爆物品、有毒物品以及管制刀具等。
乘客：好的，我知道了。
站务员：感谢您的合作。
乘客：不用谢。

## 对话 2

*乘客携带超长物品。*

安检员：对不起。按照广州地铁相关规定，乘客不可以携带超长物品进站乘车。这会影响乘客安全。
乘客：我注意一点不就行了吗？
值班站长：这关系到乘客安全，我们必须慎重。
乘客：为什么不早告诉我？
值班站长：每个出口的墙上贴有相关规定，可能您没留意。您是不是已经购票？
乘客：是啊！现在怎么办呢？
值班站长：我们给您办理退票，可以吗？
乘客：不行，玻璃这么重，我好不容易才搬进来。
值班站长：那我们让一名工作人员协助您把玻璃搬出站吧。
乘客：但我真的想坐地铁。
值班站长：对不起。但是这件事关系您和其他乘客的安全。请配合我们的工作。
乘客：好吧，我去坐公交车。
值班站长：谢谢您的理解和支持。

# Lesson 3  Epidemic Prevention Work

## Part Ⅰ  Warm up

**Discussion**

With the outbreak of COVID-19 pandemic in 2020, it has become important to prevent public health incidents. What do you think is most important for subway epidemic prevention?

## Part Ⅱ  Words and phrases

taking body temperature

wearing mask

| QR code | 二维码 | epidemic [ˌepɪˈdemɪk] | n. 流行病 |
|---|---|---|---|
| persuade [pərˈsweɪd] | vt. 劝说 | compartment [kəmˈpɑːrtmənt] | n. 隔间 |
| temperature [ˈtemprətʃər] | n. 温度 | swipe [swaɪp] | v. 扫描 |

## Part Ⅲ　Dialogue

**Topic**

Metro epidemic prevention work.

**Dialogue 1**

Persuade passengers to wear masks.

Station officer: Excuse me. According to the subway epidemic prevention requirements, please wear a mask.

Passenger: I don't have a mask.

Station officer: We have masks. Please wait a moment, I will get you one.

Passenger: No need, I'm in a hurry.

Station officer: Don't worry. It will be quick.

*The passenger ignores the station officer and prepares to go through the security check. The inspector stops the passenger.*

Inspector: Please wait. Passengers cannot enter the station without wearing a mask. There are many passengers in the station, especially in the train compartments. For the safety of the epidemic, you must wear a mask.

*The station officer takes a new mask and hands it to the passenger.*

Station officer: please wear this mask.

Passenger: OK.

Station officer: Please remember that you must wear a mask entering the subway station, otherwise you will not be able to get in the station and board the train.

Passenger: Got it.

Station officer: Thank you for your cooperation. Wish you have a happy day.

**Dialogue 2**

Ask passengers to take their temperature.

Station officer: Excuse me, please wait. According to the subway epidemic prevention requirements, we need to take your body temperature.

Passenger: No need. I'm in a hurry.

Station officer: Sorry, we must take your body temperature before you enter the station.

Passenger: No, I don't want to.

Station officer: Please cooperate with our work. There are many passengers in the station and on the trains. We need to make sure that the body temperature of each passenger is normal.

Passenger: I don't have a fever.
Station officer: That's even better. This equipment measures the temperature very quickly. You can go through the security check after the test.
Passenger: OK.
Station officer: Your body temperature is normal. Wish you have a happy ride.

## Part IV  Speaking

### Task

Create a dialogue with your partner and practice it.

### Topic

A passenger gets through the security check and refuses to swipe the health QR code. As a station officer, what will you do with it?

### Reference sentences

(1) According to the subway epidemic prevention requirements, please swipe the health QR code.

(2) Don't worry. It will be soon.

(3) Please cooperate with our work.

(4) We need to make sure that the body temperature of each passenger is normal.

(5) Otherwise you will not be able to get in the station and board the train.

### Outlines

_____
_____
_____
_____

## Part V  Exercise

### 1. Reading comprehension

A cultural and creative sales event attracted a large crowd of parents, children, and enthusiasts at the Beijing Subway's Universal Resort station over the weekend. Hosted by Beijing Top Result Metro Advertising, the two-day event aimed to showcase the allure of the Beijing subway.

Families engaged in interactive cultural activities, immersing themselves in the charm of subway culture. A variety of cultural and creative products were available on-site, including subway train models, Beijing subway commemorative ticket booklets, notebooks, keychains, and more, providing participants with a close encounter with the enchantment of subway culture.

The event not only offered a unique interactive experience for families but also served as a platform for subway enthusiasts to exhibit their interests. The event buzzed with energy, and many attendees expressed that it enhanced their understanding of subway culture, allowing them to truly appreciate the distinctive charm of subway culture firsthand.

（Source：China Daily|2024-06-04）

**Questions：**

（1）Which station was the event hosted?

（2）What were the products available on-site?

## 2. Translation

（1）您好。请扫健康二维码后再过安检。

（2）您好。请您佩戴好口罩。您的口罩佩戴错误。

（3）您好,请稍等。我们测量一下你的体温。

（4）对不起,没有佩戴口罩或未测量体温不能进站。

（5）车站是一个相对封闭的环境,请注意防疫。

# Part Ⅵ　Situation dialogue translation

### 主题

地铁防疫。

### 对话1

督促乘客佩戴口罩。

站务员：您好,根据地铁防疫要求,请您佩戴口罩。
　乘客：我没有口罩。
站务员：我们这里有口罩。您稍等,我给您拿一个口罩。
　乘客：不用了,我赶时间。

站务员：您不要着急，很快就好。

*乘客不理站务员，准备过安检。安检员拦住了乘客。*

安检员：请您稍等。不佩戴口罩不能进入车站。车站内和列车上有很多乘客。为了防疫安全，您必须佩戴口罩。

*站务员拿着一个新的口罩递给乘客。*

站务员：请您佩戴这个口罩。

乘　客：好吧。

站务员：请您记住，进入地铁车站必须佩戴口罩，否则无法进站乘车。

乘　客：知道了。

站务员：谢谢配合，祝您生活愉快。

## 对话 2

*要求乘客测量体温。*

站务员：您好，请稍等，根据地铁防疫要求，请测量体温。

乘　客：不用了，我赶时间。

站务员：对不起，进入车站前一定要测量体温。

乘　客：我不测。

站务员：请配合我们的工作。现在是疫情期间，车站内和列车上有很多乘客。我们需要确保每个乘客的体温正常。

乘　客：我没有发烧。

站务员：那更好啦，这个体温计测温很快的，测完您就可以过安检了。

乘　客：好吧。

站务员：好的，您的体温正常，祝您乘车愉快。

# Entering the Ticket Gate

Unit 5

城市轨道交通客运服务英语口语

# Lesson 1  Essential Conversations

## Part Ⅰ  Warm up

**Discussion**

As a station officer, when you see a passenger don't know how to get through the automatic gate machine(AGM), what will you do to help him?

## Part Ⅱ  Words and phrases

automatic gate machine(AGM)

QR code

| automatic gate machine(AGM) | 闸机 | gate channel | 闸机通道 |
| --- | --- | --- | --- |
| click [klɪk] | v. 点击 | | |

## Part Ⅲ  Dialogue

**Topic**

Organize passengers to enter the AGM.

**Dialogue 1**

Swipe the subway one-way ticket through the ticket gate.

Station officer: Hello everyone. Now there are many passengers passing the ticket gates, please line up and swipe your card to get through.

Passenger: How to get through the gate?

Station officer: What kind of ticket card are you using?

Passenger: The ticket was just bought at the TVM.

Station officer: This is a one-way ticket. Please hold your ticket with your right hand, and put it here at the yellow area. When you hear a sound "Di", you may enter the gate.

Passenger: Thanks a lot.

*The passenger still cannot get through.*

Station officer: Please go back a little. Stand outside the gate channel then swipe your card. Swiping the card in the gate channel cannot be sensed.

Passenger: OK, thanks.

Station officer: Please keep away your ticket. It'll be needed when you get out the destination station.

Passenger: Thank you.

Station officer: You're welcome. Have a nice trip.

**Dialogue 2**

Scan the QR code to pass the AGM.

Passenger: Hello, how can I scan the QR code to board the train?

Station officer: Please open the WeChat first, then scan this QR code on the poster.

Passenger: OK, done.

Station officer: A mini program for subway travel appears, right?

Passenger: Yes, there's a mini program.

Station officer: Click on the ride code in the small program, a QR code will appear on the phone.

Passenger: There's no QR code.

Station officer: You may use it for the first time. You need to open a password-free payment to use the ride code function for the first time.

| | |
|---|---|
| Passenger: | What? Password-free? |
| Station officer: | Yes, it is safe to pay for small amounts of money without password, relax. |
| Passenger: | OK, there's the QR code. |
| Station officer: | After you need to align the QR code of your mobile phone with the scanning frame on the side of the gate, then you can get through. |
| Passenger: | OK, thanks. |
| Station officer: | You're welcome. When you get out, open the QR code and scan again. Have a nice day. |

## Part IV  Speaking

**Task**

Create a dialogue with your partner and practice it.

**Topic**

A passenger gets through the AGM with a credit card, but he can't get through. As a station officer, what will you do to help him?

**Reference sentences**

(1) What kind of ticket card are you using?

(2) Please hold your ticket with your right hand, and put it here at the yellow area.

(3) Your credit card is insufficient.

(4) You can get charged at the ticket office.

**Outlines**

_____

_____

_____

_____

## Part V  Exercise

### 1. Reading comprehension

Ten self-service book borrowing and returning machines were installed in multiple subway stations in nine Chongqing districts to celebrate World Book Day.

The social welfare program "Palm-sized Books" offers 24-hour free book borrowing for the city's nine-to-fivers, students and tourists using subway transportation. The project was initiated by the Chongqing Municipal Culture and Tourism Commission and is jointly operated by Chongqing

Rail Transit, local public libraries and publishing institutions.

The program's launch ceremony was held on Thursday at the Zengjiayan Railway Station of Chongqing Rail Transit Line 2 in Chongqing's Yuzhong district.

According to the Chongqing Municipal Culture and Tourism Commission, 20,000 books for adults and children covering categories such as politics, economics, literature, history, geography and popular science are ready to be placed on shelves. Forty more machines will be deployed for use before the end of June,2024.

In February,2023, the southwestern municipality completed the construction of a 500-kilometer urban rail transit line, which is said to be the world's largest rail transit network in a mountainous area. The total of 50 intelligent machines in 50 subway stations across the city's CRT Line 1, 2, 3, 5, 6, 9, 10, and the Loop Line are expected to cover a passenger flow of over 100 million yearly.

The commission said that "Palm-sized Books" will also be promoted to the Chengdu-Chongqing High-Speed Railway in the future.

（Source：China Daily|2024-04-25）

**Questions**：

（1）What is the name of the social welfare program?

（2）How many intelligent machines in the subway stations?

## 2. Translation

（1）您可以打开支付宝扫码进闸。

（2）请您扫描这个二维码。

（3）您的储值卡余额不足了。

（4）您可以去自动售票机上充值,也可以去乘客服务中心充值。

（5）您可以去乘客服务中心购买充值卡。

## Part Ⅵ  Situation dialogue translation

### 主题

组织乘客进闸。

## 对话 1

*刷地铁单程票进闸。*

站务员：大家好，现在过闸乘客较多，请大家按秩序排队刷卡进闸。

乘　客：怎么进闸？

站务员：您使用的是什么票卡？

乘　客：刚刚在售票机买的票。

站务员：您这个是单程票，请右手持票，放置在闸机上方黄色读卡区域处即可，当您听到"滴"的一声，就可以进闸了。

乘　客：谢谢。

*乘客仍然不能进闸。*

站务员：请您往后退一下，站在闸机通道外方再刷卡，闸机通道内刷卡无法感应。

乘　客：好的，谢谢。

站务员：请保管好您的车票，在您的目的地站出站时您还需要用车票出站。

乘　客：谢谢。

站务员：不用谢。祝您旅途愉快。

## 对话 2

*扫描二维码过闸。*

乘　客：你好，请问怎么扫描二维码乘车？

站务员：你好，请先打开微信，扫描海报上的这个二维码。

乘　客：好的，扫好了。

站务员：然后出现了地铁出行的小程序是吗？

乘　客：是的，有一个微信小程序。

站务员：点击小程序中的乘车码，手机页面上就会出现一个二维码。

乘　客：没有出现二维码呀？

站务员：您应该是第一次使用，第一次使用需要开通免密支付才能使用乘车码功能。

乘　客：还要免密支付呀？

站务员：是的，小额免密支付是安全的，您放心。

乘　客：好的，打开二维码了。

站务员：然后您将手机二维码对准闸机侧面的这个扫描框，就可以进闸了。

乘　客：好的，谢谢。

站务员：不用谢。您出站时，再打开二维码扫描即可。祝您生活愉快。

# Lesson 2  Passengers Can't Enter the Ticket Gate

## Part Ⅰ  Warm up

**Discussion**

When you see a passenger can't enter the AGM, what will you do to help him/her as a station officer?

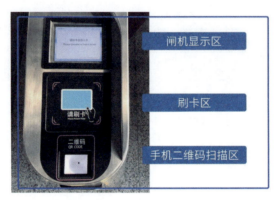

## Part Ⅱ  Words and phrases

oversized luggage gate

AGM

| oversize [ˈoʊvərsaɪz] | adj. 超大 | luggage [ˈlʌgɪdʒ] | n. 行李 |
| --- | --- | --- | --- |
| customer service center | 客服中心 | insufficient [ˌɪnsəˈfɪʃnt] | adj. 不足 |
| balance [ˈbæləns] | n. 余额 | initiative [ɪˈnɪʃətɪv] | n. 主动 |

## Part III  Dialogue

**Topic**

Passengers can't enter the AGM.

**Dialogue 1**

Insufficient balance of passenger's IC card.

A passenger is swiping his card at the AGM, but fails to get in. After several attempts, he still could not pass. The station officer takes the initiative to offer help.

Station officer: Hello, can I help you?

Passenger: Why is my card invalid?

Station officer: I see the screen of the ticket gate shows that your stored-value card balance is insufficient.

Passenger: Oh, I see. Can I recharge my card at the station?

Station officer: Of course. You can go to the customer service center to find a staff to recharge, or you can recharge your card at the TVM.

Passenger: Where is the customer service center?

Station officer: On your left, where I am pointing. Have you seen it?

Passenger: Okay, can I recharge with mobile payment?

Station officer: QR codes are available.

Passenger: OK, thanks.

**Dialogue 2**

Passengers take oversized luggage.

A passenger with oversized luggage stands in front of the ticket gate and tries to enter the gate, However, due to the baggage being too large to pass through the gate, the station officer stepped forward to provide assistance after seeing it.

Station officer: Hello, can I help you?

Passenger: My luggage is too big. I can't go through this ticket gate.

Station officer: There is a oversized luggage gate.

Passenger: where?

Station officer: Let me help you with your luggage and take you there.

*The station officer helps the passenger pick up his luggage and took him to the oversized luggage gate.*

Station officer: Right here, you can swipe your card to enter.

Passenger: Okay, it's much more convenient. Thank you very much.

Station officer: You're welcome. There are oversized luggage gates at the AGM of each station. You can find one when you get out of the ticket gate at your destination.

Passenger: OK, I see. Thanks.

Station officer: That's OK. Bye.

## Part Ⅳ  Speaking

**Task**

Create a dialogue with your partner and practice it.

**Topic**

Passengers fails to enter the gate with a student ID card.

**Reference sentences**

(1) Hello, can I help you?

(2) Why is my card invalid?

(3) This is a student ID card. Are you a student?

(4) Maybe your card is broken. You can have it checked at the customer service center.

**Outlines**

_____

_____

_____

_____

## Part Ⅴ  Exercise

### 1. Reading comprehension

According to Cao, in the park, there are vehicle manufacturers for different fields, including rail traffic, general aviation, hydrogen energy storage and transportation, as well as special mechanical equipment.

Among them is CRRC Shijiazhuang Co., which produces about 150 urban rail vehicles annually. CRRC Shijiazhuang Co. is a subsidiary company under the lead of CRRC Corporation Ltd.—the country's leading supplier for rail transit equipment. It has provided 45 trains for subways in Shijiazhuang, reaching the goal that all the trains used in the city's subway system are made locally, Cao said.

He added that the company also made more than 400 new energy buses last year.

Chery Automobile Co., a globalized automobile brand headquartered in Wuhu of Anhui Province, has established a base in the park for producing new energy cars, according to Cao.

"We will further promote more producers to gather here for developing advanced and high-end manufacturing and strive to improve the industrial chains," he said.

(Source: China Daily | 2023-07-20)

**Questions**

(1) How many urban rail vehicles does CRRC Shijiazhuang Co. produce annually?

(2) How many trains does CRRC Corporation Ltd. provide for subways in Shijiazhuang?

**2. Translation**

(1) 乘客服务中心在您右手边,向右边走100米左右就到了。

(2) 您可以使用您的手机给储值卡充值。

(3) 乘客服务中心的工作人员会告诉您如何办理。

(4) 大尺寸行李通道在旁边。

## Part Ⅵ  Situation dialogue translation

### 主题

乘客进闸失败。

### 对话1

乘客储值卡余额不足。

一名乘客在闸机处刷卡进站失败,多次尝试后仍然无法通过闸机,站务员看到后主动上前询问。

站务员: 您好,请问有什么可以帮您的吗?
乘客: 为什么我刷卡无效呢?
站务员: 我看到闸机屏幕上显示您的储值卡余额不足。
乘客: 哦,这样啊,那我在车站可以充值吗?
站务员: 当然可以,您可以去乘客服务中心找工作人员充值,也可以在自动售票机上自助充值。

乘客： 乘客服务中心在哪里？
站务员： 在您左手边，我指的地方。您看见了吗？
乘客： 好的，可以手机付款充值吗？
站务员： 现金、支付宝、微信都可以的。
乘客： 好的，谢谢。

**对话 2**

*乘客行李过大。*

*一名乘客携带大尺寸行李站在闸机前，尝试进闸。但是由于行李太大，无法通过闸机通道。站务员看到后上前提供帮助。*

站务员： 您好，您需要帮助吗？
乘客： 我的行李太大了，这个闸机通道过不去啊。
站务员： 没关系，旁边有大尺寸闸机通道。
乘客： 哪里？
站务员： 我来帮您拿行李，带您过去。

*站务员帮助乘客拿起行李，带乘客去旁边大尺寸闸机通道。*

站务员： 就是这里，您刷卡进入即可。
乘客： 好的，这样方便多了。非常感谢。
站务员： 不用谢。每个车站的闸机处都有大尺寸行李通道。您到达目的地出闸的时候可以找大尺寸闸机通道。
乘客： 好的，明白了。谢谢。
站务员： 不客气，再见。

# Lesson 3  More About Entering the AGM

## Part Ⅰ  Warm up

**Discussion**

As a station officer, what will you do if you see a passenger with a child trying to get through the AGM?

## Part Ⅱ  Words and phrases

height measuring

| height [haɪt] | n. 身高 | meter [ˈmiːtər] | n. 米 |
|---|---|---|---|
| measure [ˈmeʒər] | v. 测量 | soldier [ˈsoʊldʒər] | n. 士兵 |
| dedicate [ˈdedɪkeɪt] | vt. 奉献 | register [ˈredʒɪstər] | v. 注册 |

## Part Ⅲ　Dialogue

**Topic**

**Dialogue 1**

Passenger gets through the AGM with a child .

when station staff see a passenger with a child who is taller than 1. 2 meters, they should come to ask the passenger to buy the child ticket.

Station officer: Good morning sir. May I ask how tall is your child? Your child could take the subway free if his height is less than 1. 2 meters.

Passenger: Yes, he is.

Station officer: OK, please come here and we need to check.

*The station staff takes them to measure the child's height and finds out he is taller than 1. 2 meters.*

Station officer: Sorry. He is taller than 1. 2 meters. He cannot take the subway free, please buy him a ticket.

Passenger: OK.

Station officer: Thank you for your cooperation.

**Dialogue 2**

Passengers take the subway free.

Passenger: Hello, I am a serviceman on active duty. Can I take the subway for free?

Station officer: Sure. Please show me your soldier ID.

Passenger: Here it is.

Station officer: Okay, please wait a moment, let me register.

*The station officer registers the relevant information of the ticket-free person in the ticket-free registration book.*

Station officer: Hello, please come with me.

Passenger: I don't need to go through the ticket gate?

Station officer: No, we have a dedicated free passenger entrance.

Passenger: OK.

*The station officer opens the free passenger entrance to allow the passenger to enter.*

Station officer: You can enter this green channel. When you arrive at your destination, find a green channel like this as well, then show your soldier ID to the station officer to get out for free.

Passenger: OK, thank you.

## Part Ⅳ  Speaking

**Task**

Create a dialogue with your partner and practice it.

**Topic**

A passenger older than 70 comes to take subway for free.

**Reference sentences**

(1) Hello, I am 71 years old. Can I take the subway for free?

(2) Okay, please wait a moment. Let me register.

(3) Sure. Please show me your ID.

(4) We have a dedicated free passenger entrance.

**Outlines**

_____

_____

_____

_____

## Part Ⅴ  Exercise

**1. Reading comprehension**

Beijing vigorously promoted the development of green transportation, extending the total mileage of rail transit lines to 1,172 km by September, 2023, giving the city first-place ranking in China, according to a senior city official on Thursday.

"Beijing currently has 27 urban rail transit lines with a length of 807 km and four suburban railways with a length of 365 km," said Gao Peng, deputy mayor of Beijing, at the fifth session of the Standing Committee of the 16th Beijing Municipal People's Congress in January, 2023.

The city actively promoted new-energy vehicles on the roads. The number of new-energy and clean-energy vehicles accounts for 94 percent of public buses in the city, while 65 percent of the city's taxi cars are pure-electric vehicles.

Gao said the government will continue to shorten the transfer distance of public transport in efforts to optimize green transportation services in the city proper, where the target for green travel is 76.5 percent by the end of 2025.

(Source: China Daily | 2023-09-21)

**Questions**

(1) How many urban rail transit lines does Beijing currently have?

(2) What is the target for green travel in Beijing by the end of 2025?

**2. Translation**

(1) 请出示您的证件。

(2) 请走这个免费通道。

(3) 请稍等,我需要登记您的相关信息。

(4) 从这个通道进入即可乘车。

## Part Ⅵ  Situation dialogue translation

**主题**

更多进闸情况。

### 对话 1

乘客与儿童一同进闸。

当站务员发现一乘客带着身高超过1.2米的儿童时,上前要求乘客为儿童买票。

站务员: 早上好。请问您的孩子身高多少?如果您的小孩儿身高不到1.2米,他可以免费乘坐地铁。

乘客: 他身高不到1米。

站务员: 请跟我来,我们这里有测身高的。

站务员带两名乘客到测身高的地方测试之后发现这个小孩身高超过1.2米。

站务员: 对不起。他超过1.2米了,他不能免费乘坐地铁,请为他买一张票吧。

乘客: 好的,那我去买票。

站务员: 好的,谢谢合作。

### 对话 2

乘客免票。

乘客: 您好,我是一名现役军人,请问可以免票乘坐地铁吗?

站务员: 是的,请出示您的士兵证。

乘客： 这里。
站务员： 好的,请稍等,我登记一下。
*站务员在免票登记簿上登记免票人员相关信息。*
站务员： 你好,请跟我来。
乘客： 不用过闸机吗?
站务员： 不用,我们有专门的免费乘客通道。
乘客： 好的。
*站务员打开免费乘客通道,让乘客进入。*
站务员： 您从这个通道进入就可以乘车了。您到达目的地时,同样找到这样的通道,出示证件让站务员给您开门即可。
乘客： 好的,谢谢。

# Conversations on Platform

Unit 6

城市轨道交通客运服务英语口语

# Lesson 1  Preserving Order on Station Platform

## Part I  Warm up

**Discussion**

When there are too many passengers at the platform, what should you do to keep order as a station officer?

## Part II  Words and phrases

platform

screen door

| keep order | 维护秩序 | screen door | 站台门 |
|---|---|---|---|
| organize [ˈɔːrgənaɪz] | v. 组织 | confusion [kənˈfjuːʒn] | n. 混乱 |
| row [roʊ] | n. 队列 | convenient [kənˈviːniənt] | adj. 方便 |

## Part III  Dialogue

**Topic**

Organize passengers to wait for the train in order.

**Dialogue 1**

Organize passengers to wait in line.

*When there are too many passengers on the platform causing confusion in the waiting, the station operator should organize the passengers to queue up.*

Station officer: Please stand in two rows on both sides of the screen door. Sir, please stand behind this passenger.

Passenger: Why? I came first.

Station officer: You are standing in the middle of the door, This is the area for passengers to get off the train. Alight first, board later.

Passenger: I should be ahead of him.

Station officer: Please cooperate with us. It's convenient for everyone and you can get on the train faster.

Passenger: All right.

Station officer: Thank you for your cooperation.

**Dialogue 2**

Passenger forced boarding the train while the doors are closing up.

*The doors are closing up.*

Station officer: Passengers, the doors are closing up. Please have some patience wait for the next train. Stay within the yellow safety line. Thanks for your cooperation. Sir, it's very dangerous. Please wait for the next train.

Passenger: That serious? I am in a hurry for work. I could be late.

Station officer: I see. But still, you cannot board at the last second especially when the doors are already closing up. It's very dangerous. The next train is coming in 5 minutes. Please wait.

Passenger: All right.

Station officer: Thanks for your cooperation.

## Part IV  Speaking

**Task**

Create a dialogue with your partner and practice it.

## Topic

There is a passenger in a wheel chair at the platform.

**Reference sentences**

(1) Please stand in two rows on both sides of the screen door.

(2) Please let this passenger get on the train first.

(3) Please make room for us.

(4) Let me help you to get on the train.

**Outlines**

___

___

___

___

## Part V    Exercise

**1. Reading comprehension**

The Canal Culture and Food Festival was held at the renowned Sen Long Restaurant this month to showcase the signature dishes of Huaiyang cuisine to diners in Beijing.

Sen Long Restaurant was established in Beijing in 1924 by Zhang Sanlong from Jiangsu Province. The initial location of the restaurant changed because of subway construction in 2005, and it was reopened in Dongcheng district in 2019.

(Source: China Daily | 2023-09-11)

**Questions**

(1) Why did the initial location of the restaurant change?

(2) Where did the restaurant reopen?

**2. Translation**

(1) 请大家站成两排有序候车。

(2) 您好,请排队候车。

(3) 您好,请不要倚靠站台门。

(4) 您好,请站在黄线外候车。

## Part VI  Situation dialogue translation

**主题**

组织乘客有序候车。

### 对话 1

组织乘客排队候车。

*站台上乘客很多造成候车混乱时,站务员组织乘客排队候车。*

站务员: 请大家站在车门两边排成两列候车。这位先生,请您排在这位乘客后面。

乘　客: 为什么呢? 我先来的。

站务员: 您站在车门中间了,这里是车上乘客下车区。先下后上。

乘　客: 我应该排在他前面。

站务员: 请您配合我们的工作,这样方便大家,您也可以更快上车。

乘　客: 好吧。

站务员: 谢谢合作。

### 对话 2

在车门即将关闭时,阻止强行上车的乘客。

*列车即将关闭。*

站务员: 各位乘客,车门即将关闭,没有上车的乘客请耐心等候下一趟车。请不要越出黄色安全线。谢谢合作。先生,您这样做很危险。请您等下一列车。

乘　客: 有那么严重? 我赶时间。我上班要迟到了。

站务员: 您的心情我能理解,但是为了您的安全,请您千万不要抢上正在关门的列车,真的很危险。下列车将于 5 分钟后进站,请耐心等待。

乘　客: 好吧。

站务员: 谢谢合作。

# Lesson 2  Services under Special Circumstances

## Part I  Warm up

**Discussion**

As a station officer, what will you do when you see a passenger leans against the screen door?

## Part II  Words and phrases

rail line area

half-height screen door

| | | | |
|---|---|---|---|
| lean [liːn] | v. 倚靠 | half-height screen door | 半高站台门 |
| slippery [ˈslɪpəri] | adj. 滑的 | restrain [rɪˈstreɪn] | vt. 约束 |
| pillar [ˈpɪlər] | n. 核心 | registration [ˌredʒɪˈstreɪʃn] | n. 登记 |

## Part Ⅲ  Dialogue

**Topic**

Special circumstances at the platform.

**Dialogue 1**

Children on the platform chase and fight.

Station officer: Hello, kids! The ground is slippery and easy to fall. Please do not run on the platform.

*The child ignores the station operator.*

Station officer: Whose children are they?

Passenger: Mine. What's up?

Station officer: Please restrain your children so that they do not run and fight on the platform.

Passenger: Just two kids. It's okay.

Station officer: There are many pillars on the platform. They may hit a pillar during the run and get hurt. Also there are many passengers on the platform, as well as the elderly, pregnant women, etc., They may hit someone and hurt them.

Passenger: It's not that serious.

Station officer: For the children themselves and other passengers, please restrain your children.

Passenger: OK.

Station officer: Thank you for your cooperation.

**Dialogue 2**

A passenger drops something in the rail line.

*A passenger drops her goods in the rail line area and asks the station officer for help.*

Passenger: Excuse me. I drop my keys off in the rail line area. What can I do now? Can you help me to pick it up?

Station officer: Sure. We can help you, but we need to check its location first.

*After checking its location, the station officer does not think it will endangers the train operation. However, there are too many passengers crowding around. He decides to pick it up after the train service is closed.*

Station officer: Madam, we can pick it up for you, but not now. It has to wait till the train service is closed.

Passenger: Why not now?

Station officer: It's peak time. If I try to get down there right now, I might interfere with the train running and cause a for delay everyone's travel. Thanks for your understanding.
Passenger: So what can I do now?
Station officer: You can come with me to the customer service center for a registration. Leave your contact there and we will call you when we get your keys back, OK?
Passenger: All right.

## Part IV  Speaking

### Task
Create a dialogue with your partner and practice it.

### Topic
A passenger drops her cellphone in the rail line area at the platform, she asks station officer to get the phone back immediately.

### Reference sentences
(1) Sure we can help you but we need to check its location first.
(2) We can pick it up for you, but not now. It has to wait till the train service is closed.
(3) It will affect our operation.
(4) You have to come with me to the customer service center for a registration.

### Outlines

_____
_____
_____
_____

## Part V  Exercise

### 1. Reading comprehension

As the number of foreign tourists increased in Beijing recently, the capital's subway authorities initiated a pilot program to install multilingual language translation machines in some subways stations.

"The first group consisted of eight machines," the local government said on Wednesday.

Machines have been installed at eight stations: Tian'anmenxi (Line 1), Dongzhi Men (Line 2), Beijing Railway Station (Line 2), Nanluogu Xiang (Line 6), Olympic Park (Line 8),

Xi'erqi (Line 13), Maquanying (Line 15) and Universal Resort (Line 7) and Batong Line.

The machines can support translations in Chinese, English, Japanese and Korean, ensuring convenient communication for passengers of different nationalities.

Meanwhile, to further meet the travel needs of both Chinese and foreign tourists, the Beijing subway is providing specialized English training for station personnel.

(Source: China Daily|2024-03-28)

**Questions**

(1) How many machines did the first group consisted?

(2) What languages can the machines support for translations?

## 2. Translation

(1) 您好,请您照顾好您的孩子,不要在站台上奔跑。

(2) 我明白手机对您的重要性,但是现在是地铁运营客流高峰期,无法为您捡手机。

(3) 您跟我到客服中心登记。明天一早通知您来领取手机。

(4) 站台乘客太多,小朋友乱跑很危险。

# Part Ⅵ  Situation dialogue translation

### 主题

站台特殊情况。

### 对话 1

站台上儿童追逐打闹。

站务员: 小朋友,你好!地面很滑,容易摔倒,请不要在站台上奔跑。

小朋友不理站务员。

站务员: 请问这是谁家的孩子?

乘客: 我家的,怎么了?

站务员: 请您照顾好您的孩子,让他们不要在站台上奔跑打闹。

乘客: 小孩子嘛,没事的。

站务员: 站台上有很多柱子,小朋友在奔跑中可能会撞到柱子,伤到自己。其次,站台上很多乘客,还有老年人、孕妇等,小朋友撞到人,会造成对方受伤。
乘　客：没那么严重的。
站务员：为了小朋友自己,也为了其他乘客,请您约束您的孩子。
乘　客：好吧。
站务员：谢谢合作。

### 对话 2

*乘客有物品掉入轨行区。*

*乘客物品掉入轨行区,寻求站务员帮助。*

乘　客：你好,我钥匙掉入轨行区了,怎么办呢？您能帮我捡回来吗？
站务员：可以的,但是我得先看看钥匙掉的位置。

*站务员查看物品掉落位置后,认为掉落物品不影响行车。现在乘客较多,准备结束运营后拾取。*

站务员：女士,钥匙可以帮您捡回来,但是现在不能捡,得结束运营以后才能捡。
乘　客：为什么现在不能捡？
站务员：现在正是客流高峰期,如果下去捡拾物品会影响列车运行,耽误大家出行。请您谅解。
乘　客：那我怎么办呀？
站务员：请同我一起到客服中心登记,留下您的联系方式。捡回钥匙我们会立刻联系您的,您看可以吗？
乘　客：好吧。

# Lesson 3 Platform Accident

## Part Ⅰ  Warm up

**Discussion**

A passenger rushes to get on the train, while the screen doors are closing. As a station officer, what you should do?

## Part Ⅱ  Words and phrases

| clamp [klæmp] | v. 夹 | emergent [iˈmɜːrdʒənt] | adj. 紧急的 |
|---|---|---|---|
| notify [ˈnoʊtɪfaɪ] | vt. 通知 | colleague [ˈkɑːliːɡ] | n. 同事 |
| urgent [ˈɜːrdʒənt] | adj. 紧急的 | arrival [əˈraɪvl] | n. 到达 |

## Part III  Dialogue

**Topic**

Emergency at the platform.

**Dialogue 1**

One passenger is clamped by the platform doors and gets hurt.

*Due to equipment faults, a passenger gets clamped by the screen doors. The station officer takes emergent actions immediately and the doors are opened.*

Station officer: We are sorry that you are scared. Are you hurt?

Passenger: It really hurts. (Pointing to a certain part of his body.)

*The station officer notifies the duty station master to take care of it.*

Duty Station Master: Do you need to go to the hospital?

Passenger: It hurts a lot. (Pointing to a certain part of his body.)

Duty Station Master: Please contact your family. My colleague will take you to the hospital together with your family.

**Dialogue 2**

The train is delayed.

Passenger: Excuse me, can you tell me when is the next train arriving?

Station officer: We are just informed that the next train could be late for ten or more minutes.

Passenger: I have got something urgent to deal with. I really need to go right now. Any help here?

Station officer: In that case, the best choice is to change to other transportation. Please follow our direction when exiting the station. You can have your tickets handled at any metro station in 7 days. Thanks for your understanding and cooperation.

Passenger: All right.

*The passenger leaves the station.*

## Part IV  Speaking

**Task**

Create a dialogue with your partner and practice it.

**Topic**

A passenger is clamped with the screen doors while the doors are closing.

**Reference sentences**

(1) We are sorry that you are scared. Are you hurt?

(2) Please don't rush into the train while the doors are closing.

(3) How are you? Do you need to go to the hospital?

**Outlines**

_____

_____

_____

_____

## Part V　Exercise

### 1. Reading comprehension

Beijing plans to introduce the Beijing Pass, an all-in-one card to enhance the convenience of subway travel for foreign visitors, as part of the city's ongoing efforts to make transportation more friendly to international travelers.

The card is expected to be available for sale at seven major train stations and two airports in the city, helping foreign passengers easily access Beijing's rail transit system.

To improve payment convenience for foreign passengers, all 335 stations across the 17 lines managed by Beijing Subway have been equipped with point-of-sales machines as of June 1, 2024. These machines allow foreign passengers to purchase tickets and pay for rides using international bank cards. Additional services will gradually be provided, such as allowing MasterCard and other international cards to be used for gate access, single-trip, and supplementary ticket purchases.

（Source：China Daily | 2024-07-31）

**Questions：**

(1) What is the Beijing Pass?

(2) What has the Beijing Subway done to improve payment convenience for foreign passengers?

### 2. Translation

(1) 为了您的安全，车门关闭时，请不要上下列车。

(2) 非常抱歉，列车晚点了，您可以选择乘坐其他交通工具。

(3) 由于列车晚点，需要退票的乘客可在七日内完成退款。

(4)您受伤了吗？需要去医院吗？

## Part VI　Situation dialogue translation

**主题**

站台紧急事件。

**对话 1**

站台门夹人导致受伤。

*由于设备故障，地铁站台门夹到乘客。站务员采取应急处理，打开站台门。*

站务员：　您好，让你受惊了！请问你受伤没有？

乘客：　我这里很痛。（乘客指着身体某处。）

*站务员立刻通知值班站长处理。*

值班站长：　要不要去医院检查一下。

乘客：　我这里很疼。（乘客指着身体某处。）

值班站长：　您给家里人打个电话，我找同事和您家人一同陪您去医院检查检查。

**对话 2**

列车晚点。

乘客：　请问下一趟列车还要等多长时间？

站务员：　刚才接到通知，下一趟列车可能要晚点十几分钟。

乘客：　我有急事，怎么办呢？

站务员：　请您改乘其他交通工具。请按照工作人员的指引离开车站。您的车票 7 日内可到地铁各站办理相关票务手续。感谢您的谅解与合作。

乘客：　好的。

*乘客离开站台。*

# Getting Out of the Ticket Gate

Unit 7

城市轨道交通客运服务英语口语

# Lesson 1  Organization of Passengers at the Ticket Gate

## Part Ⅰ  Warm up

**Discussion**

As a station officer, what will you do if you see a passenger can't get out of the AGM with a one-way ticket?

## Part Ⅱ  Words and phrases

special treatment certificate

one-way ticket

| organization [ˌɔːrɡənəˈzeɪʃn] | n. 组织 | special treatment | 特殊待遇 |
|---|---|---|---|
| certificate [sərˈtɪfɪkət] | n. 证书 | safety line | 安全线 |
| recycling slot | 回收口 | confirm [kənˈfɜːrm] | v. 确认 |

## Part Ⅲ   Dialogue

**Topic**

Organize passengers to exit the ticket gate.

**Dialogue 1**

Passengers use one-way tickets.

*The station officer saw a passenger who does not know how to put in a one-way ticket.*

Passenger: How to exit the gate?

Station officer: What kind of ticket are you using?

Passenger: A one-way ticket.

Station officer: Please stand outside the yellow safety line, hold the ticket in your right hand and put the one-way ticket into the recycling slot.

Passenger: Just put the ticket in?

Station officer: Yes, we will recycle the one-way ticket. After you put in the ticket into the AGM, the ticket gate will open up, then you can get out.

Passenger: OK, thank you.

Station officer: You are welcome.

**Dialogue 2**

Ticket-free passengers exit the AGM.

*When a ticket-free passengers exit the ticket gate, the station officer should confirm the certificate and register the information and then open the side door to let them go out.*

Passenger: Hello, I am a ticket-free passenger. How can I get out?

Station officer: Hello, please show me your ID.

Passenger: I'm older than 65.

Station officer: Please show me your special treatment certificate.

Passenger: OK, here.

Station officer: Please wait a moment. I'll register your information. Please wait for me here.

Passenger: OK.

Station officer: Please come with me. I will take you out through the side door.

## Part Ⅳ   Speaking

**Task**

Create a dialogue with your partner and practice it.

**Topic**

A passenger with oversize luggage comes to exit the ticket gate.

**Reference sentences**

(1) Please come with me. I will take you to the oversized luggage gate.

(2) Please wait a moment. I'll help you recycle the one-way ticket.

(3) What kind of ticket are you using?

(4) I'll help you swipe your card. Wait a moment please.

**Outlines**

_____

_____

_____

_____

## Part V  Exercise

**1. Reading comprehension**

Visiting cities across China in recent years, I have found myself, more often than not, using the subway, instead of hailing a cab or taking a bus ride, to travel from one place to another. With high frequency, punctuality, fast speed and reasonable fair, subways have become the preferred mode of transport for both local commuters and tourists.

Statistics show that by the end of last year, more than 50 Chinese cities had subways—with dozens more on the waiting list—covering a total length of more than 9,000 km. Beijing and Shanghai, each having 900 km of subways, have been leading, interchangeably, the global subway network for the past decade. Chengdu, the capital of Sichuan Province, epitomizes the development of subways in China. The host of the ongoing FISU World University Games (Universiade), Chengdu opened its first subway line in 2010. Today, it has 12 operational lines covering 500 km. Eight more lines are under construction in the city, better known for its cuisine and giant pandas.

(Source: China Daily | 2023-08-01)

**Questions:**

(1) Why the subways have become the preferred mode of transport for both local commuters and tourists?

(2) When did Chengdu open its first subway line?

**2. Translation**

(1) 请将您的单程票投入闸机口,我们需要回收单程票。

(2)如果您需要纪念票,请到客服中心购买。

(3)请出示您的老年优待证。

(4)请稍等,我需要登记您的信息,登记好后我带您从边门出去。

## Part VI　Situation dialogue translation

**主题**

组织乘客出闸。

### 对话 1

乘客使用单程票。

站务员看到有位乘客不知道如何投入单程票。

乘客：　请问怎么出闸?
站务员：　您使用的是什么票?
乘客：　单程票。
站务员：　请您站在黄线外,右手持票,将单程票投入闸机回收口/投票口。
乘客：　放进去就可以出去了吗?
站务员：　是的,单程票我们是要回收的。您将票投入闸机后,闸机打开您就可以出去了。
乘客：　好的,谢谢。
站务员：　不用谢。

### 对话 2

免票乘客出闸。

免票乘客出闸时,站务员应确认登记后打开边门,让其出去。

乘客：　你好,我是免票乘客,请问怎么出去呢?
站务员：　您好,请出示您的证件。
乘客：　我是65岁以上的老年人。
站务员：　请您出示老年人优待证。
乘客：　好的,这里。
站务员：　请稍等,我登记一下您的信息,您在这里等我。
乘客：　好的,谢谢。
站务员：　好了,您跟我来,我带您从边门出去。
乘客：　好的,谢谢。

# Lesson 2  Passengers Can't Get Out of the Ticket Gate

## Part Ⅰ   Warm up

**Discussion**

A passenger fails to exit the AGM, what you should do to help him as a station officer?

## Part Ⅱ   Words and phrases

ticket booth

one-way ticket

| policy [ˈpɑːləsi] | n. 政策 | considerate [kənˈsɪdərət] | adj. 体贴的 |
|---|---|---|---|
| display [dɪˈspleɪ] | v. 显示 | make up | 补充 |
| previous [ˈpriːviəs] | adj. 以前的 | | |

## Part Ⅲ  Dialogue

**Topic**

A passenger fails to exit.

**Dialogue 1**

A passenger losts ticket.

Station officer: Hello, can I help you?

Passenger: How do I get out?

Station officer: Have you swiped your card yet?

Passenger: No, I can't find the ticket.

Station officer: What kind of ticket do you have?

Passenger: One-way ticket.

Station officer: Are you sure you can't find the ticket?

Passenger: Yes, I really can't find it.

Station officer: In this case, it should be dealt with as a lost ticket.

Passenger: I got on the subway at Xunlimen Station.

Station officer: Since you don't have a ticket, we can't be sure of your starting point. You need to pay for the entire trip that is 8 yuan.

Passenger: I don't think so. I already bought a ticket, and I only took the train for four stops.

Station officer: Sorry. I believe that you accidentally lost it, but this is the subway rule. Please be considerate and take good care of your ticket next time.

Passenger: Fine.

Station officer: Thank you for your cooperation.

**Dialogue 2**

Passengers cannot leave the station due to overtravel.

Station officer: Hello. How can I help you?

Passenger: The ticket keep returning back from the slot. why?

Station officer: Please hand it to me to take a check.

*The Station officer checks the gate display screen.*

Station officer: The gate display screen shows that the ticket value is insufficient. Your ticket value is 2 yuan, but it costs 3 yuan from the Apple Garden Station to the Fuxingmen Station. Please make up one yuan.

Passenger: Where can I make up the ticket?

Station officer: Go straight and turn right, then you can see a ticket booth. You can give your ticket to the staff and pay 1 yuan and then you can get out of the gate.
Passenger: OK, thank you.
Station officer: You're welcome. You won't miss it.

## Part IV  Speaking

### Task
Create a dialogue with your partner and practice it.

### Topic
A passenger can't get out of the gate because of a oversized luggage. As a station officer, what can you do to help him?

### Reference sentences
(1) You can get out through the oversized luggage gate.

(2) Please follow me. It's not far away.

(3) Please swipe your card at the ticket gate first then come with me.

### Outlines

_____

_____

_____

_____

## Part V  Exercise

### 1. Reading comprehension

Before I interviewed Ma Tuo, I never realized that there were police rooms in subway stations.

Instead, I thought that officers would be rushed from a nearby police station in the event of any problems on the underground rail network.

Ma told me that two police officers are assigned to large or high-traffic stations, while smaller stations host one officer.

During rush hours, the officers patrol the stations, while the rest of the time, they are on call in the police room.

"Having police rooms in subway stations ensures that officers can arrive at the scene as quickly as possible. Compared with quarrels or fights in communities, similar conflicts in the confined subway, especially during peak commuting periods, can escalate more quickly, making passengers angrier or more emotional," Ma said.

（Source：China Daily | 2023-07-25）

### Questions

（1）How many police officers are assigned to large or high-traffic stations?

（2）During rush hours, the officers patrol the stations, what are they doing while the rest of the time?

### 2. Translation

（1）您的储值卡余额不足了，需要充值后才能出站。

（2）如果您的储值卡丢失的话，您需要补办票卡后再刷卡出站。

（3）地铁关于丢失单程票出站的规定是补足全额车票才可出站。

（4）请不要着急。您在您的包里仔细找一下，也可以明天到车站失物招领处问询。

## Part Ⅵ　Situation dialogue translation

### 主题

乘客出闸失败。

### 对话 1

乘客车票丢失。

站务员：您好，请问有什么需要帮忙？
　乘客：我该怎么出去？
站务员：您刷卡了吗？
　乘客：没有，我找不到车票了。
站务员：您是什么车票？
　乘客：单程票。
站务员：您确定找不到车票了吗？
　乘客：的确找不到了。

站务员： 这种情况的话,要按照遗失车票的情况处理。
乘客： 我是在循礼门站上车的。
站务员： 由于您没有车票,因此我们无法确定您的起点,您需要补交全程票款 8 元。
乘客： 我买了票的,而且我只坐了 4 站。
站务员： 对不起。我相信您是不小心丢失的,但这是地铁运营管理规定,请您体谅。下次请保管好您的车票。
乘客： 好吧。
站务员： 感谢配合。

## 对话 2

*乘客超程不能出站。*

站务员： 您好。有什么能帮您吗?
乘客： 车票从投币口投入,为什么会退出来?
站务员： 请让我检查一下。

*站务员查看闸机显示屏。*

站务员： 闸机显示屏显示票价不足。您的车票余额是 2 元,从苹果园站到复兴门站需要 3 元。请补 1 元。
乘客： 去哪里补票呢?
站务员： 前面右转有一个票亭,您可以把您的票给工作人员,交钱补票后再出闸。
乘客： 好的,谢谢。
站务员： 不客气。你不会错过的。

# Lesson 3  Passengers Against Regulations

## Part Ⅰ  Warm up

**Discussion**

If a passenger stride across the gate without swiping a ticket, what will you do as a station officer?

## Part Ⅱ  Words and phrases

ticket evasion

tickets for elderly

| stride [straɪd] | v. 骑 | ticket evasion | 逃票 |
|---|---|---|---|
| escape [ɪˈskeɪp] | v. 逃跑 | purchase [ˈpɜːrtʃəs] | 购买 |
| student ticket | 学生票 | stored-value card | 储值卡 |

## Part III  Dialogue

### Topic 1
Passengers escape tickets.

**Dialogue 1**

Passengers escape tickets by crossing the gate without swiping ticket or scanning the payment code.

*The station officer notices a passenger attempting to cross the gate without swiping ticket or scanning the payment code.*

| | |
|---|---|
| Station officer: | Hello, please do not cross the gate. Enter the station by using your ticket. |
| Passenger: | I didn't buy a ticket. |
| Station officer: | You can use the ticket machine to buy tickets, or scan the payment code to enter the station. |
| Passenger: | I don't have any money. |
| Station officer: | The subway cannot be taken for free. Please purchase your ticket before entering the station. |
| Passenger: | May I buy the ticket next time? |
| Station officer: | Please get off the gate, otherwise I have to inform the security. |
| Passenger: | Okay. |
| Station officer: | The subway prohibits ticket evasion. Please purchase a ticket to enter the train. |

**Dialogue 2**

An adult uses a student ticket.

*A station officer discovers an adult using a student ticket to enter the station.*

| | |
|---|---|
| Station officer: | Sir, you are not allowed to use a student ticket. |
| Passenger: | I didn't use a student ticket. |
| Station officer: | What you are using now is a student ticket, which is different from the ordinary stored-value card. |
| Passenger: | This is my daughter's card. |
| Station officer: | Please purchase a subway ticket. Obviously, you are not a student and you cannot use a student card. |
| Passenger: | Can't I use my child's ticket? |
| Station officer: | Your child can use a student ticket, but as an adult, you cannot use a |

| | student ticket. |
|---:|:---|
| Passenger: | Okay, where can I buy the ticket? |
| Station officer: | You can use the TVM over there to buy tickets, or you can swipe the QR code to enter the station. |
| Passenger: | Alright, I see. |
| Station officer: | Thank you for your cooperation. Wish you have a good day. |

**Topic 2**

Passengers carry children into the station.

**Dialogue 1**

A passenger brings a child who doesn't exceed the height limit.

| Passenger: | Hello, can my child take the subway for free? |
|---:|:---|
| Station officer: | Good morning, Sir. If your child is less than 1.2 meters tall, he can take the subway for free. |
| Passenger: | Yes, he is less than 1.2 meters tall. |
| Station officer: | Okay, please follow me. |

*The station officer takes two passengers to the height measurement area and finds out that the child is indeed less than 1.2 meters tall.*

| Station officer: | Yes, he can take the subway for free. I will assist you in passing the gate. |
|---:|:---|
| Passenger: | Thank you. |
| Station officer: | You're welcome. |

**Dialogue 2**

A passenger brings a child who exceed the height limit.

*A station officer finds a passenger carrying a child over 1.2 meters in height. He approaches and asks the passenger to buy a ticket for the child.*

| Station officer: | Good morning, Sir. If your child is less than 1.2 meters tall, he can take the subway for free. |
|---:|:---|
| Passenger: | Yes, he is less than 1.2 meters tall. |
| Station officer: | Okay, please follow me. |

*The station officer takes them to the height testing area and finds out that the child is over 1.2 meters tall.*

| Station officer: | Sorry, Sir. He is over 1.2 meters tall and cannot take the subway for free. Please buy him a ticket. |
|---:|:---|
| Passenger: | Okay. |
| Station officer: | Thank you for your cooperation. |

## Part Ⅳ  Speaking

**Task**

Create a dialogue with your partner and practice it.

**Topic**

A passenger tries to get through the ticket gate without wiping tickets or scanning the payment code. As a station officer, what will you do to stop him?

**Reference sentences**

(1) Hello, please do not cross the gate.

(2) You can use your phone to scan the QR code and enter the station.

(3) Ticket evasion is a violation of subway company regulations.

(4) If you insist, I will inform the security.

**Outlines**

_____

_____

_____

_____

## Part Ⅴ  Exercise

**1. Reading comprehension**

As China enters sanfu—the three 10-day periods on the Chinese lunar calendar that are expected to be the hottest of the year—some major cities have devised creative ways to help residents keep cool.

In Chongqing, for example, the subway officer has set up rest areas inside 113 stations, which are kept around 25℃, ideal havens from the heat. These areas are located in quiet corners of the spacious stations. Each one is equipped with chairs, water dispensers and a first-aid kit, and anyone nearby, not just passengers, can come inside to cool off.

"We provide help for people overcome by the heat," said Zhan Yan, a subway station manager in the city. "We have medicated oil and traditional Chinese medicines for heatstroke."

People using the rest areas can ask station staff members for help at any time, Zhan added.

(Source: China Daily | 2023-07-18)

**Questions**

(1) What does the subway officer set up inside 113 stations in Chongqing?

(2) What is the stations equipped with for the people to cool off?

**2. Translation**

(1) 请您购买车票进站。地铁公司禁止逃票行为。

(2) 您可以在自动售票机上购买车票,也可以刷二维码进站。

(3) 请问您的孩子身高是多少? 您不确定的话请到这里测量。

(4) 在成年人监护陪同下,身高不足1.2米(含)的儿童可免费乘车。

## Part Ⅵ  Situation dialogue translation

### 主题1
乘客逃票。

### 对话1
乘客跨越闸机逃票。
*站务员在闸机处发现一名乘客试图翻越闸机。*
站务员: 你好,请不要翻越闸机。请检票进站。
　乘客: 我没有买票。
站务员: 您可以使用自动售票机购买车票,或者扫描支付码进站。
　乘客: 我没有钱。
站务员: 地铁不能免费乘坐,请您购票后再进站。
　乘客: 我下次再买票吧。
站务员: 请退出闸机,否则我只能通知安保人员了。
　乘客: 好吧。
站务员: 地铁禁止逃票行为。请购票乘车。

### 对话2
成年人使用学生票。
*站务员发现一名成年人使用学生票进站。*

站务员： 先生,您不能使用学生票。
乘客： 我没有用学生票啊。
站务员： 您现在使用的就是学生票,学生票和普通储值卡是不一样的。
乘客： 这是我女儿的卡。
站务员： 请您购买一张地铁票。您显然不是学生了,不能使用学生卡。
乘客： 我用我孩子的票也不行吗?
站务员： 您的孩子可以使用学生票。但是作为成年人,您不能使用学生票。
乘客： 好吧,那我去哪里买票?
站务员： 您可以使用那边的自动售票机买票,也可以刷二维码进站。
乘客： 好吧,知道了。
站务员： 谢谢合作,祝您生活愉快。

**主题2**

乘客携带儿童进站。

### 对话1

乘客携带免票儿童进站。

乘客： 你好,我的小孩可以免费坐地铁吗?
站务员： 早上好,先生。您的小孩儿如果身高不到1.2米,他可以免费乘坐地铁。
乘客： 是的,他身高不到1.2米。
站务员： 好的,请跟我来。
站务员带他们到测身高的地方测试之后发现这个小孩身高的确不到1.2米。
站务员： 是的,他可以免费乘坐地铁。我来协助你们过闸机。
乘客： 谢谢。
站务员： 不用谢。

### 对话2

乘客携带超高儿童进站。

站务员发现一乘客带着身高超过1.2米的儿童。他上前要求乘客为儿童买票。

站务员： 早上好,先生。您的小孩儿如果身高不到1.2米,他可以免费乘坐地铁。
乘客： 是的,他身高不到1.2米。
站务员： 好的,请跟我来。
站务员带他们到测身高的地方测试之后发现这个小孩身高超过1.2米。
站务员： 对不起,先生。他超过1.2米了,他不能免费乘坐地铁。请为他买一张票吧。
乘客： 好的。
站务员： 谢谢合作。

## PartⅦ  Tongue twister

(1)A big black bear sat on a big black bug.

(2)A big black bug bit a big black bear and made the big black bear bleed blood.

(3)A big black bug bit a big black dog on his big black nose!

(4)A loyal warrior wail rarely worry why we rule.

(5)A noise annoys an oyster, but a noisy noise annoys an oyster more!

(6)Ann and Andy's anniversary is in April.

(7)Bake big batches of bitter brown bread.

(8)Big black bugs bleed blue black blood but baby black bugs bleed blue blood.

(9)Black background, brown background.

(10)Blake's black bike's back brake bracket block broke.

(11)Blue glue gun, green glue gun.

(12)Caution: Wide Right Turns.

(13)Each Easter Eddie eats eighty Easter eggs.

(14)Elizabeth has eleven elves in her elm tree.

(15)Elizabeth's birthday is on the third Thursday of this month.

# Information Service

Unit 8

城市轨道交通客运服务英语口语

# Lesson 1  Passengers Asking for Directions

## Part Ⅰ  Warm up

**Discussion**

As a station officer, what will you do when a passenger asks for a direction which you don't know?

## Part Ⅱ  Words and phrases

map

subway entrance

| | | | |
|---|---|---|---|
| map [mæp] | n. 地图 | turn left | 左转 |
| destination [ˌdestɪˈneɪʃn] | n. 目的地 | trip [trɪp] | n. 旅途 |
| line [laɪn] | n. 线路 | square [skwer] | n. 广场 |

## Part Ⅲ  Dialogue

**Topic**

Routine enquiry.

**Dialogue 1**

A passenger enters a subway line on which the destination station is located.

Passenger: Excuse me, I'd like to go to Guanggu Square.

Station officer: You could buy a ticket to Guanggu Square Station. Get out of the station at exit A, then turn left (or right) for 500 meters to your destination.

Passenger: Thank you very much.

Station officer: You're welcome. Have a nice trip.

**Dialogue 2**

A passenger enters a subway line on which the destination station is not located.

Passenger: Excuse me, I'd like to go to Guanggu Square.

Station officer: You could buy a ticket to the Xunlimen Station. Transfer metro line 2 directed to Guanggu Square Station, then get out of Guanggu Square Station at exit A, then turn left (or right) for 500 meters to your destination.

Passenger: Thanks.

Station officer: You're welcome. Have a nice trip.

## Part Ⅳ  Speaking

**Task**

Create a dialogue with your partner and practice it.

**Topic**

A passenger asks how to go to the nearest hospital.

**Reference sentences**

(1) You can get out of the station at exit A, then turn left.

(2) You should take the subway to the station ×××.

(3) What can I do for you?

(4) Are you OK? Do you need assistance in calling 120?

**Outlines**

_____

_____

_____

_____

## Part V  Exercise

### 1. Reading comprehension

Official data showed that the number of passenger trips handled by China's urban rail transit networks surged 40 percent year-on-year in September.

The Ministry of Transport said 2.49 billion passenger trips were made via China's urban transit networks in 55 cities in september, 2023.

The figure was 24.9 percent higher than the average monthly level in 2019.

Two new urban rail transit lines were added nationwide during September, bringing the total number of transit lines to 299, according to the ministry.

（Source：China Daily|2023-10-11）

**Question**：

How many new urban rail transit lines were added nationwide during September?

### 2. Translation

（1）您可以从出口 E1 出站,然后向右走五百米就可到达目的地。

（2）您还需要继续搭乘地铁列车到×××站,才能到达。

（3）从地铁出站后您还需搭乘 720 路公交车。

（4）公交车站在地铁出口右边 100 米处。

## Part VI  Situation dialogue translation

### 主题

线路问询。

### 对话 1

乘客进入目的地车站所在地铁线路。

乘客： 你好,我想去光谷广场

站务员： 您可以买一张到光谷广场站的车票,下车后,在 A 口出站,向左边（或右边）走 500 米,就可以到您要去的地方。

乘客： 谢谢。

站务员： 不用谢,祝你旅途愉快!

**对话 2**

乘客进入非目的地车站所在地铁线路。

乘　客： 你好,我想去光谷广场。

站务员： 您可以买一张到循礼门站下车的车票。在循礼门车站换乘 2 号线光谷广场方向列车。在光谷广场站 A 口出站,向左边(或右边)走 500 米,就可以到您要去的地方。

乘　客： 谢谢。

站务员： 不用谢,祝你旅途愉快!

# Lesson 2  Lost and Found

## Part Ⅰ  Warm up

**Discussion**

As a station officer, what will you do when a passenger tells you that his mobile phone is lost in the metro station?

## Part Ⅱ  Words and phrases

certificates

| lost and found | 失物招领 | certificate [sərˈtɪfɪkət] | n. 证件 |
| --- | --- | --- | --- |
| mobile phone | 手机 | briefcase [ˈbriːfkeɪs] | n. 公文包 |
| passport [ˈpæspɔːrt] | n. 护照 | property [ˈprɑːpərti] | n. 财产 |

## Part III  Dialogue

**Topic**

Dealing with the lost items.

**Dialogue 1**

A passenger losts his briefcase.

Passenger: Could you help me?
Station officer: Yes. What seems to be the problem?
Passenger: I left my briefcase in the station. I wonder if anyone has turned in it.
Station officer: Sorry, your briefcase hasn't been turned in.
Passenger: Then what shall I do?
Station officer: Don't worry, you can dail the subway service hotline for help.
Passenger: OK. Thank you.

**Dialogue 2**

A passenger losts his passport.

Passenger: Excuse me. Could you help me?
Station officer: Yes. What seems to be the problem?
Passenger: Well, I wonder if anyone has turned in a passport.
Station officer: I am afraid not. Have you lost your passport?
Passenger: I think so. I remember the last place I used it yesterday was in the station.
Station officer: Where exactly did you use your passport in the station?
Passenger: In the ticket center.
Station officer: Well. Let me check if they have found a passport.

*A minute later.*

Station officer: Sorry. Your passport hasn't been turned in there.
Passenger: What shall I do?
Station officer: You can fill in this lost property report. I will keep my eye out for it. Those kinds of things usually turn up eventually, but I suggest you contact your embassy and tell them about your situation, so they can issue you a new passport in case it com't be found.
Passenger: You are right. Do you have a pen?
Station officer: Here you are.

**Dialogue 3**

A passenger inquires at the lost property office.

| | |
|---|---|
| Station officer: | Lost property. Can I help you? |
| Passenger: | Yes, please. I lost my briefcase. |
| Station officer: | Would you mind telling me some details clearly? |
| Passenger: | Well, it's light brown and got two buckles at the front. |
| Station officer: | What did you have inside the briefcase? |
| Passenger: | Some important documents, pens and a novel. |
| Station officer: | All right. When and where did you lose the briefcase? |
| Passenger: | Well, It's about 5:10 p.m. I washed my hands and my briefcase was next to me at the washroom. |
| Station officer: | Ok. Please give me your contact number. |
| Passenger: | Yes. I'm Jason Smith. My contact number is ××××××. |
| Station officer: | OK. we will contact you if we find your briefcase. |
| Passenger: | Thanks a lot. |
| Station officer: | My pleasure. |

## Part Ⅳ  Speaking

**Task**

Create a dialogue with your partner and practice it.

**Topic**

A passenger losts her passport in the station.

**Reference sentences**

(1) Where did you use your passport in the station?

(2) You can fill in this lost property report. I will keep my eye out for it.

(3) Would you mind telling me some details clearly?

(4) When and where did you lose it?

**Outlines**

_____

_____

_____

_____

## Part Ⅴ  Exercise

### 1. Reading comprehension

Southwest China's Chongqing municipality is allowing farmers to carry large baskets on subway trains during peak hours. The farmers are allowed to use Line 4, dubbed the "Vegetable Basket Line", every day. They may carry baskets on their backs or in a small cart, or balance two baskets with a pole on their shoulders. The baskets, made of bamboo, are usually filled with fresh vegetables.

Some netizens commented on the local government's inquiry platform recently that the city should prohibit passengers from carrying large items, including the baskets, during peak hours because they can hinder other passengers when space is especially limited.

Chongqing Rail Transit responded that passengers can carry items on the subway as long as the sum of the length, width, and height does not exceed 2 meters and the weight does not exceed 20 kilograms. The Line 4 allowance has not only warmed the hearts of a large number of farmers, but also the general public.

"This is what a modern city should be—the farmers who carry baskets and those nine-to-fivers who carry laptops are essentially no different," one netizen commented.

To make things more convenient for passengers, station staff members usually open the gates a few minutes earlier, use handheld metal detectors for security checks, guide farmers to take the elevators in the subway and help them lift their baskets onto the train.

（Source：China Daily|2024-03-25）

**Questions：**

(1) What is the second name of Line 4 of Chongqing Rail Transit?

(2) What kind of items can be carried into the subway in Chongqing?

**2. Translation**

(1) 请问您还记得在什么地方、什么时间丢失了您的包吗？

(2) 您能提供更详细的信息吗？

(3) 您的包里都有一些什么物品呢？

(4) 您可以到失物招领处查看，如果没有的话也可以到失物招领处登记信息。

# Part VI  Situation dialogue translation

**主题**

处理遗失物品。

### 对话 1

乘客丢失公文包。

乘客：你能帮我个忙吗？

站务员：怎么了？

乘客：我的公文包落在了车站。我想知道是否有人上交一个包。

站务员：不好意思，没有人上交。

乘客：那我该怎么办呢？

站务员：不要担心，你可以拨打地铁服务热线求助。

乘客：谢谢！

### 对话 2

乘客丢失护照。

乘客：你能帮我个忙吗？

站务员：可以，怎么了？

乘客：请问是否有人上交一个护照？

站务员：没有。您的护照丢了？

乘客：是的。我记得我使用护照的最后一个地方是这个车站。

站务员：你在车站具体哪个地方使用了？

乘客：售票处。

站务员：好的。我打电话问一下售票处是否有人发现护照。

1 分钟以后。

站务员：不好意思，那里没有人上交护照。

乘客：那我该怎么办呢？

站务员：您填一下失物登记表，我会帮你留意的。这类物品被人捡到的话一般最后会被上交的。但是建议您联系大使馆，告诉他们您的情况，那样如果您的护照一直没有找到，他们会发一个新的给您。

乘客：你说得对。你这里有笔吗？

乘务员：给您。

### 对话 3

乘客在失物招领处询问。

站务员： 失物招领处。有什么能帮您的?
乘客： 你好,我的公文包丢了。
站务员： 您能说得具体一些吗?
乘客： 淡棕色的,前方有两个扣子。
站务员： 公文包里都有什么。
乘客： 一些重要的文件、钢笔、一本小说。
站务员： 好的。什么时候以及在哪里丢的?
乘客： 下午五点十分左右,我在洗手间洗手的时候公文包还在我旁边。
站务员： 好的。方便留下您的联系方式吗?
乘客： 我叫杰森·史密斯,我的电话号码是××××××。
站务员： 好的。我们找到您的公文包的话会联系您。
乘客： 谢谢。
站务员： 不客气。

# Lesson 3  Passengers Asking for Help

## Part Ⅰ  Warm up

**Discussion**

As a station officer, what will you do if you see a passenger pass out?

## Part Ⅱ  Words and phrases

automated external defibrillator (AED)

smart first aid station

| first aid | 急救 | AED | 自动体外心脏除颤器 |
|---|---|---|---|
| smart first aid station | 智能急救站 | headache [ˈhedeɪk] | n. 头疼 |
| round-the-clock | 日夜不停地 | dizzy [ˈdɪzi] | 眩晕 |

## Part Ⅲ  Dialogue

**Topic**

Handle sick passengers.

**Dialogue 1**

The station officer finds a passenger who look ill.

Station officer: Hello. I am the Station officer. You look ill. Are you OK?

Passenger: Oh, I feel chest pain, dizzy and can hardly breathe.

Station officer: Let me see what I can do to relieve your pain. It seems that you are suffering a heart attack. Do you have any medicine with you?

Passenger: Yes. It's in my right pocket.

Station officer: OK. I will bring you a cup of water, so you can take medicine.

*The station officer brings a cup of water as soon as possible. A moment later after the passenger takes medicine.*

Station officer: Do you feel better now?

Passenger: Yes. I feel much better. Thank you for your help.

Station officer: My pleasure. Let me take you to the station master's office for a rest.

Passenger: Thank you very much.

**Dialogue 2**

A passenger comes for help because another passenger get sick.

Passenger: Help! Please!

Station officer: What's the matter with him?

Passenger: Oh, he suddenly faints. Please help him.

Station officer: Calm down. Let me call an ambulance for him right now.

Passenger: Hurry up. Thank you.

Station officer: OK. The ambulance is coming soon. Let him lie lower. Also, we need to loosen his tie and collar.

Passenger: That's very kind of you.

*The doctor is coming.*

Doctor: Time is life. Let me check for a pulse. Apply CPR for him.

Passenger: I really appreciate.

Station officer: It's my pleasure.

Doctor: It's my pleasure.

Information Service | Unit 8 | 137

## Part IV  Speaking

**Task**

Create a dialogue with your partner and practice it.

**Topic**

A passenger gets hurt in the station and bleeds.

**Reference sentences**

(1) How do you get hurt? Do you need me to call the 120?

(2) Here is a band aid, please use it.

(3) This is a band aid. Do you need me help you to put it on?

**Outlines**

_____

_____

_____

_____

## Part V  Exercise

**1. Reading comprehension**

From birthday wishes and dating profiles to resumes, a variety of personalized advertisements have been popping up on electronic screens called lightboxes in metro stations in Guangzhou.

"Personalized advertisements not only bring a sense of novelty to people's daily commutes but provide a platform for self-expression for many 'e-people', a popular internet term referring to individuals with outgoing personalities," said Li Jing, a marketing manager with Guangzhou Metro Media Co. The company has so far completed over 100 such ads. "The original intention was to create an interactive platform between subway media and the passengers," Li said.

It has become one of the top trending topics on Chinese social media since netizens began sharing multiple screenshots of personal ads posted in subway stations, with many featuring distinctive content such as resumes and dating profiles.

(Source: China Daily | 2023-06-14)

**Questions:**

(1) What are the electronic screens called on which the personalized advertisements have been popping up?

（2）What is the original intention of the personalized advertisements?

## 2. Translation

（1）你好,你现在感觉怎么样?

（2）您需要我帮您叫救护车吗?

（3）这是创可贴,您需要我帮您贴上吗?

（4）请注意安全。这是急救箱,请让我帮您处理一下伤口。

## Part Ⅵ　Situation dialogue translation

**主题**

### 对话1

站务员发现乘客生病。

站务员：　你好,我是站务员,你看起来不舒服,还好吗?
　乘客：　我感觉胸痛、眩晕、呼吸困难。
站务员：　我看一下怎么缓解您的疼痛。你似乎心脏病发作。你身上带药了吗?
　乘客：　嗯,在我右边的口袋里。
站务员：　嗯,拿到了,我去倒杯水让你吃药。
站务员尽可能快地为乘客倒了一杯水。乘客服药后,过了片刻。
站务员：　您感觉好点了吗?
　乘客：　嗯,我感觉好多了。谢谢你的帮助。
站务员：　不客气,我带你去站长办公室休息一下吧。
　乘客：　谢谢。

### 对话2

乘客寻求帮助。

　乘客：　救命!
站务员：　他怎么了?
　乘客：　他忽然昏倒了,请帮一下他。
站务员：　镇定,我来叫救护车。
　乘客：　请快一点,谢谢。

站务员： 嗯，救护车正在过来，让他躺得低一点，我们松一下他的衣领和领带。
乘客： 你真是太好了。

*医生来了。*

医生： 时间就是生命，让我来测一下他的脉搏，使用心肺复苏术。
乘客： 很感谢。
站务员： 不客气。
医生： 不客气。

# Lesson 1  Station Daily and Equipment Failure Broadcast

## Part Ⅰ  Warm up

**Discussion**

As a station officer, what will you broadcast if the train gets late?

station officer

## Part Ⅱ  Words and phrases

broadcasting equipments

| broadcasting equipments | 广播设备 | vehicle [ˈviːəkl] | n. 车辆 |
|---|---|---|---|
| occupy [ˈɑːkjupaɪ] | v. 占领 | track [træk] | n. 轨道 |
| violator [ˈvaɪəleɪtə(r)] | n. 违反者 | scatter [ˈskætər] | v. 扔 |

## Part Ⅲ  Broadcast Content

**Topic 1**

Platform broadcasting.

**Practice**

(1) Your attention please! Please stand in line to get on the train, and let passengers get off first. No boarding while the light is flashing and the door is closing.

(2) Watch out for the door as it is closing, and be careful not to get caught.

(3) Walk towards the middle of vehicle after boarding. Try not to occupy the position near the door. Thank you!

(4) The train is arriving. This train is bound for Sihui Station.

(5) Please let passengers get off first and keep away from the platform screen door. Thank you for your cooperation.

(6) Please stand behind the yellow safety line while waiting for the train. Please stand back from the doors. Please take care of your belongings. If you drop something into the track, please contact the station officer.

(7) Your attention please! please offer your seat to anyone in need. Thank you!

(8) Your attention please! The train heading for the direction of Olympic Sport Center is coming. Please mind the gap between the train and platform while boarding the train.

(9) For your safety, please stand back from the platform screen door while waiting for the train.

(10) Dear passengers, please take care of your children and belongings. No running, chasing and fighting in the platform.

(11) No rushing, please.

(12) Please don't squat.

(13) Passengers heading for the Gym, please pay attention, as the front of the train is rather crowded, please go to the back of the train. Thank you for your cooperation!

(14) Your attention please! Please move along the platform to the middle of the train for easier boarding. In order to keep the environment clean and healthy, please don't smoke or litter on the trains or platform. Thank you for your cooperation!

**Topic 2**

Reminding broadcasting.

**Practice**

(1) Your attention please!

Inflammable, explosive or poisonous items are strictly prohibited anywhere in the station. The violator shall be sent to the police station if the violation is substantial.

(2) Your attention please!

For safety reasons, please use the lift if you have oversized baggage.

Thank you for your cooperation!

(3) Your attention please!

For your safety, when traveling on escalators, stand firm and hold the handrail.

Please do not run or walk in the wrong direction.

(4) Your attention please!

Smoking, spitting and scattering rubbish in the station or the train are prohibited so as to keep these places clean.

Take good care of the facilities in station and comply with *instructions of passengers*. It is forbidden to beg and sell any commodities.

Thank you for your cooperation!

### Topic 3

Last train service broadcasting.

**Practice**

(1) Your attention please! The last train to Guanggu Square Station is arriving.

The last train for Guanggu Square Station will depart at 23:00. Please prepare for boarding.

(2) Your attention please!

This is the last train to Guanggu Square Station.

Please board immediately.

(3) Your attention please!

Train service for today has ended. Please leave the station immediately.

Thank you.

### Topic 4

Malfunction of subway equipments.

**Practice**

(1) Your attention please!

Please follow the station officers' directions to enter as the ticket gates are not working.

We apologize for any inconvenience.

(2) Your attention please!

Please follow the guidance of the station officers to exit as there is something wrong with the ticket gates.

The one-way ticket should be given to the station officer for recycling. Passengers with stored-value tickets should pay the fare within 7 days at any station.

We apologize for any inconvenience.

(3) Your attention please!

Please buy tickets at the customer service center as the TVM are not working.

We apologize for any inconvenience.

(4) Your attention please!

Some escalators are not in use because of a problem with the power supply.

We apologize for any inconvenience.

(5) Your attention please!

Station lighting is under emergency repair, but trains are still running.

Please contact the station officer if you need any assistance.

We apologize for any inconvenience.

(6) Your attention please!

The breakdown has been repaired. We apologize for any inconvenience.

Have a nice trip.

**Topic 5**

Train broadcasting.

Practice

(1) Welcome to subway Line 2. This train is bound for Guanggu Square Station. The next station is Guanggu Square Station. The door on the left side will be used. Please keep away from the door, and get ready for your arrival.

(2) To keep a clean and healthy environment, do not eat, drink, smoke or throw litter on the train. Thank you.

(3) The next station is Hongshan Square Station. Please get ready for your arrival, and make sure you have all your belongings with you. Hongshan Square Station is a transfer station. Passengers go for Line 4, please prepare to get off.

(4) We are arriving at Hongshan Square Station. Welcome to take this line on your next trip. Have a nice day.

(5) Please offer your seats to anyone in need. Thank you.

# Part Ⅳ  Speaking

**Task**

Create a dialogue with your partner and practice it.

**Topic**

Inform passengers to come to the station control room?

**Reference sentences**

(1) May I have your attention please?

(2) Mr ×××, if you hear this broadcast please come to the station control room at the

station hall.

**Outlines**

_____
_____
_____
_____

## Part V  Exercise

**1. Togue twister**

(1) Can you can a can as a canner can can a can?

(2) I wish to wish the wish you wish to wish, but if you wish the wish the witch wishes, I won't wish the wish you wish to wish.

(3) I scream, you scream, we all scream for ice-cream!

(4) How many cookies could a good cook cook if a good cook could cook cookies? A good cook could cook as much cookies as a good cook who could cook cookies.

(5) The driver was drunk and drove the doctor's car directly into the deep ditch.

**2. Translation**

(1) 各位乘客请注意！请×××小朋友到车站控制室。您的家人在找您。

(2) 请站台上的小朋友不要奔跑。请父母照顾好自己的孩子。

(3) 各位乘客，请注意安全，往后站，在候车区内候车。

(4) 为了您的安全，候车的时候请勿倚靠站台门。

## Part VI  Situation dialogue translation

**主题1**

站台广播。

**练习**

(1) 各位乘客请注意！请排队候车，先下后上，灯闪关门时请勿上车。

(2) 车门关闭时，请小心车门，谨防被夹。

(3) 上车后往车厢中部走，尽量不要站在门口处。谢谢！

(4) 列车即将到达。本次列车前往四惠站。

(5) 请先让乘客下车，远离站台门。谢谢您的配合。

(6) 请站在黄色安全线内候车。请勿靠近车门。请妥善保管您的随身物品。如果您的物品掉落轨道，请与工作人员联系。

(7) 各位乘客请注意！请把座位让给有需要的乘客。谢谢！

(8) 各位乘客请注意！前往奥体中心的列车即将进站。上车时，请小心列车与站台之间的空隙。

(9) 为了您的安全，候车时请勿倚靠站台门。

(10) 尊敬的乘客，请照顾好您的孩子，保管好随身物品。严禁在站台上奔跑、追逐打闹。

(11) 请勿拥挤。

(12) 请勿蹲姿候车。

(13) 前往体育馆的乘客请注意，由于车头较拥挤，请往列车尾部走。谢谢您的配合！

(14) 请注意！请大家沿着站台前行，从列车中部上车。为了保持清洁、健康的候车环境，请勿在列车和车站吸烟和乱扔垃圾。谢谢您的配合！

### 主题 2

提醒广播。

### 练习

(1) 各位乘客请注意！

携带易燃、易爆、有毒的危险物品进站乘车，属于违法行为，一经发现将被移交公安部门处理。

(2) 各位乘客请注意！

为了您和其他乘客的安全，如携带大件行车请使用直梯。

谢谢您的配合！

(3) 各位乘客请注意！

为了您的安全，搭乘扶梯时，请站稳扶好。

请勿奔跑、逆行。

(4) 各位乘客请注意！

请保持环境卫生，禁止在车站或列车上吸烟、吐痰和乱扔垃圾。

请爱护站内设施，遵守《乘客须知》。禁止乞讨、兜售商品等行为。

谢谢您的配合！

### 主题 3

末班车广播。

### 练习

(1) 各位乘客请注意！开往光谷站的末班车即将进站。

开往光谷站的末班车将于 23:00 由本站开出。请准备乘车。

(2)各位乘客请注意!

本次列车是开往光谷站方向的末班车。

请您尽快上车。

(3)各位乘客请注意!

今天的列车服务已经终止,请尽快出站。

谢谢。

## 主题 4

设备故障广播。

### 练习

(1)各位乘客请注意!

因车站闸机故障,请听从工作人员的指引进站。

给您带来不便,敬请谅解。

(2)各位乘客请注意!

因车站闸机故障,请听从工作人员的指引出站。

请将单程票交给工作人员回收。持储值票的乘客请在 7 日内到任意车站补交本次车费。

给您带来不便,敬请谅解。

(3)各位乘客请注意!

因车站自动售票机故障,请到车站客服中心购买车票。

给您带来不便,敬请谅解。

(4)各位乘客请注意!

由于电力供应故障,部分电扶梯无法使用。

给您带来不便,敬请谅解。

(5)各位乘客请注意!

车站照明系统紧急抢修中,列车正常运行。

如有困难请联系工作人员。

给您带来不便,敬请谅解。

(6)各位乘客请注意!

故障已解除。给您带来不便,敬请谅解。

祝您旅途愉快。

## 主题 5

列车广播。

### 练习

(1)欢迎乘坐地铁 2 号线。这趟列车开往光谷广场站。下一站是光谷广场,列车开启左侧车门。请勿靠近车门,并提前做好下车准备。

(2)为了保持清洁和健康的环境,禁止在列车上饮食、抽烟或扔垃圾。谢谢。

(3)列车运行前方是洪山广场站。请提前做好下车准备,带好随身物品。洪山广场可换乘4号线。需要换乘的乘客请准备下车。

(4)列车即将到达洪山广场站。欢迎您下次再次乘坐本地铁线路。祝你有美好的一天。

(5)请给有需要的人让座。谢谢。

# Lesson 2  Broadcast for Train Delayed

## Part Ⅰ  Warm up

**Discussion**

As a station officer, what will you do if a passenger asks you how to exit when the ticket gates are shut down in emergency?

## Part Ⅱ  Words and phrases

| | | | | | |
|---|---|---|---|---|---|
| delay [dɪˈleɪ] | v. 延迟 | malfunction [ˌmælˈfʌŋkʃn] | n. 故障 |
| power supply | 供电 | suspend [səˈspend] | vt. 暂停 |
| crowd [kraʊd] | adj. 拥挤的 | technical [ˈteknɪkl] | adj. 技术的 |

## Part Ⅲ  Broadcast Content

**Topic 1**

Irregular train service.

**Practice**

Delay service.

(1) Dear passengers, we are sorry to inform you that the current train heading for ××× Station will be delayed for a short time. We apologize for any inconvenience.

(2) Your attention please! We are sorry to inform you that there will be a short delay for the train to ×× station because of malfunction of power supply / malfunction of signal equipment/

train equipment failure /rail equipment failure/ passenger flow/ the weather. If you are in a hurry, you can change other transport. Please follow the guidance of station staff. Passengers with stored-value tickets should pay the fare within 7 days at any station. Thank you for your understanding and cooperation.

(3) Your attention please! There will be a short delay. Please accept our apologies.

(4) Your attention please! This train to Qingdao station will not stop at Licun station.

(5) Your attention please! There will be a delay of 5 minutes because the large passengers flow at Gongzhufen Station. We apologize for any inconvenience this might cause.

(6) Your attention please! There will be a delay before the doors open because of technical fault. Thank you for your cooperation.

**Topic 2**

Passenger flow organization at the station hall when large passenger flow coming up for the delay of trains.

**Practice 1**

Feeder bus service.

Your attention please!

We are sorry to inform you that train service to ×× station is suspended because of malfunction of power supply/ malfunction of signal equipment / train equipment failure /rail equipment failure/ passengers flow/ the weather.

We have informed the feeder bus. Passengers go to the assigned bus waiting place at Exit 2, and free buses will be available.

Please follow the guidance of the station officer while exiting.

Thank you for your understanding and cooperation.

**Practice 2**

Train service is temporarily suspended.

Your attention please!

Train service between ×× station and ×× station is disrupted because of the weather.

Please take other transport and follow the guidance of station officer while exiting.

Fare will not be deducted when you exit.

We apologize for any inconvenience.

**Practice 3**

Some ticket gates for entering are temporarily shut down.

Your attention please!

Crowded management plans are now in operation as the station is too crowded. Some entry gates are temporarily shut down. Please use other ticket gates which are sill on.

We apologize for any inconvenience.

**Practice 4**

Passengers get into the station in batches.

Dear passengers, crowded management plans are now in operation as the station is too crowded. Please follow the directions to enter the station in batches.

If you are in a hurry, please take other transport.

We will give you further information as soon as possible.

Thank you for your understanding and cooperation.

**Topic 3**

Platform service for large passenger flow.

**Practice 1**

Transfer station.

Your attention please!

Crowded management plans are now in operation as the transfer passengers are too crowded. Please walk in batches and leave the platform as soon as possible.

Please take other transport if you are in a hurry. Please accept our apologies for any inconvenience.

**Practice 2**

Passengers board and alight on platform.

Attention, please!

Please follow the direction of the station officer, stand along the platform screen doors. Please leave a passage in the middle of the train door for passengers to get off. Please exit the train first and then board. Take care of yourself.

Boarding passengers, please move towards the middle of the carriage and do not gather at the door.

Thank you for your cooperation.

## Part IV  Speaking

**Task**

Create a dialogue with your partner and practice it.

**Topic**

How to broadcast train malfunction?

**Reference sentences**

(1)We are sorry to inform you the train to ×××  is delayed.

(2)Please be patient and wait.

**Outlines**

 

 

 

 

## Part V　Exercise

**1. Tongue twister**

(1)Peter Piper picked a peck of pickled peppers.

(2)A peck of pickled peppers Peter Piper picked.

(3)If Peter Piper picked a peck of pickled peppers.

(4)Where's the peck of pickled peppers Peter Piper picked？

(5)I thought a thought, but the thought I thought wasn't the thought I thought I thought.

**2. Translation**

(1) 各位乘客请注意！由于即将进站的列车出现故障,请您耐心等待。

(2) 故障会尽快处理,请您耐心等待。

(3) 各位乘客请注意！本次列车稍有延误。为您带来不便,敬请谅解。

(4) 各位乘客请注意！由于车站内过于拥挤,车站正在进行客流控制,部分入站闸机暂时关闭。给您带来不便,敬请谅解。

## Part VI　Situation dialogue translation

**主题1**

非正常列车运行。

**练习**

延误服务。

(1)各位尊敬的乘客,我们抱歉地通知您,本站开往××方向列车将出现短时延误。给您带来不便,敬请谅解!

（2）各位乘客请注意！我们抱歉地通知您,由于供电设备故障/信号设备故障/列车设备故障/轨道设备故障/客流原因/天气原因,本站开往××方向列车将出现短时延误。有急事的乘客,请改乘其他交通工具。请按照工作人员的指引出站。持储值票的乘客请在7日内到任意车站补交本次车费。感谢您的理解与配合。

（3）各位乘客请注意！本次列车将出现短时延误,敬请谅解。

（4）各位乘客请注意！本次开往青岛站方向的列车将在李村站不停车通过。

（5）各位乘客请注意！由于在公主坟站出现大客流,本次列车将延误5分钟。给您带来不便,敬请谅解。

（6）各位乘客请注意！由于技术故障,车门将稍迟打开,请勿倚靠站台门。谢谢您的配合。

### 主题2

列车延误产生大客流时站厅客流组织。

### 练习1

接驳公交服务。

各位乘客请注意！

我们抱歉地通知您,由于供电设备故障/信号设备故障/列车设备故障/轨道设备故障/客流原因/天气原因,本站开往××方向列车运行暂时终止。

我们已经通知接驳公交。请乘客从本站的2号出口出站,到指定的候车地点换乘免费公交车。

请按照工作人员的指引出站。

感谢您的理解与配合。

### 练习2

列车运行暂时中止。

各位乘客请注意！

由于天气原因,××站到××站间列车运行暂时中止。

请改乘其他交通工具。

出闸时,不扣车费。

给你带来不便,敬请谅解。

### 练习3

部分进站闸机暂时关闭。

各位乘客请注意！

由于车站内过于拥挤,车站正在进行客流控制。部分进站闸机暂时关闭。

给您带来不便,敬请谅解。

**练习 4**

乘客分批进站。

各位乘客,由于客流较大,车站正在进行客流控制。请听从车站工作人员指引,分批进站乘车。

如有急事,请改乘其他交通工具。

有进一步的消息,我们会尽快通知大家。

谢谢您的理解与配合。

**主题 3**

大客流时站台客流组织。

**练习 1**

换乘站。

各位乘客请注意!

由于换乘客流较大,现在进行客流控制。

请分批换乘,尽快离开站台。

如有急事,请改乘其他交通工具。给你带来不便,敬请谅解。

**练习 2**

乘客上下车。

各位乘客请注意!

请听从站务员指引,沿着站台门排队站好。请在车门中间留出下车通道。请先下后上。注意安全。

上车乘客请往车厢中间走,不要在车门处聚集。

谢谢您的配合。

# References

[1] 程逆.城市轨道交通客运服务英语口语[M].北京:人民交通出版社股份有限公司,2017.

[2] 颜景林.城轨交通客服英语口语100例.[M].2版.北京:科学出版社,2016.

[3] 程钢.城市轨道交通专业英语(运营管理方向)[M].北京:电子工业出版社,2016.

[4] 伍帅英,应婷婷.轨道交通英语口语实训教程[M].大连:大连理工大学出版社,2015.

[5] 李建民.城市轨道交通专业英语[M].2版.北京:机械工业出版社,2016.

[6] 王笑然,于伯良.城市轨道交通专业英语[M].北京:中国电力出版社,2017.

[7] 杨国平.城市轨道交通实用英语[M].北京:外语教学与研究出版社,2012.

[8] 兰云飞.城市轨道交通服务英语[M].北京:北京交通大学出版社,2014.

[9] 郭冬梅,康平平.轨道交通行业英语[M].成都:西南交通大学出版社,2016.